OFF THE RAILS

ALSO BY BEPPE SEVERGNINI

Ciao, America!

La Bella Figura

OFF

the

RAILS

A Train Trip Through Life

BEPPE SEVERGNINI

TRANSLATED BY
ANTONY SHUGAAR

BERKLEY
NEW YORK

BERKLEY
An imprint of Penguin Random House LLC
1745 Broadway, New York, NY 10019

Copyright © 2019 by Beppe Severgnini
Translation copyright © 2019 by Antony Shugaar
Penguin Random House supports copyright. Copyright fuels creativity,
encourages diverse voices, promotes free speech, and creates a vibrant culture.
Thank you for buying an authorized edition of this book and for complying
with copyright laws by not reproducing, scanning, or distributing any part of it
in any form without permission. You are supporting writers and allowing
Penguin Random House to continue to publish books for every reader.

BERKLEY and the BERKLEY & B colophon are registered trademarks of
Penguin Random House LLC.

Library of Congress Cataloging-in-Publication Data

Names: Severgnini, Beppe, author. | Shugaar, Antony, translator.
Title: Off the rails : a train trip through life / Beppe Severgnini ;
translated by Antony Shugaar.
Other titles: Signori, si cambia. English.
Description: First edition. | New York : Berkley, 2019. |
Translation of: Signori, si cambia.
Identifiers: LCCN 2018033020| ISBN 9781592408726 (hardcover) |
ISBN 9780698162112 (ebook)
Subjects: LCSH: Severgnini, Beppe--Travel. | Voyages and travels. | Railroad travel.
Classification: LCC G465 .S46813 2019 | DDC 910.4--dc23
LC record available at https://lccn.loc.gov/2018033020

First Edition: February 2019

Printed in the United States of America
1   3   5   7   9   10   8   6   4   2

Jacket art: train by patrimonio designs ltd;
train ticket by NMV; background map by Bardocz Peter
Jacket design by Rita Frangie
Book design by Kristin del Rosario

33614080881294

To Giles Watson

CONTENTS

-INTRODUCTION-

The Therapy of the Rails

xi

-1-

From Washington to Washington: With Antonio Across America

1

-2-

From Berlin to Palermo: A Vertical Europe

43

-3-

From Moscow to Lisbon: A Horizontal Europe

59

-4-

From Sydney to Perth: The Indian Pacific

83

-5-

From the Atlantic to the Pacific: Last Train for Obama

95

-6-

From Trieste to Trapani: Italy in Second Class

127

-7-

Trans-Siberian Express: Honeymoon for Four

149

-8-

From the Baltic to the Bosphorus: The Last Summer of Communism

159

-9-

From Naples to London: Across Europe with Little Donald

177

-10-

What to Bring

185

ACKNOWLEDGMENTS

201

INDEX OF PLACES

203

The Therapy of the Rails

I felt for the first time all the sweetness of life
In a compartment of the North Express,
between Wirballen and Pskow.

—VALERY LARBAUD, *POEMS OF A. O. BARNABOOTH*

Does it even make sense to write and read about trains and travel at a time like this? When the world is changing and people are in constant movement? Certainly: now more than ever. While we travel, we think; we exercise our thoughts; we check our ideas in the eyes of a stranger. It becomes clear that the world is more than just the grim reports on the television news, that it's a daily surprise and enterprise. You need to get out and see the world if you want to understand it. The intolerant are often ignorant and lazy; let's get them moving. Let's convince them to take a trip.

Of all the different kinds of travel, the one I like best is the old kind, gradual, both private and social: train travel. A trip that appears to be a straight line. In fact, though, it's the most surprising kind of travel. There couldn't be anything better if what we're interested in is the curves of the world.

There are two categories of train lovers: those who watch trains and those who board them and depart. Trainspotters and train travelers. I found this distinction in the preface to a handsome illustrated book published in 1980, *Great Railway Journeys of the World*, based on a BBC documentary series. Personally, I've never had doubts on the matter. Trains are like friends and restaurants: you have to experience them.

I've gone around the world in installments. Every trip has been a revelation. I watched regions, nations, and continents change moods and colors, and I've met more people on trains than in forty years of airplane flights. Every train trip has been a spectacle; come to think of it, so has every train traveler. Trains are stages, cafés, bazaars. The only talk show that will never go off the air is the one that buzzes with conversation, every single day, along the tracks of Italy, Europe, and the world at large. The characters repeat themselves—the liberal and the conservative, indignant or resigned, young and old, the intelligent young woman and the muscle-bound young man without much to say—but the plot changes, as does the backdrop. Familiarity, almost inevitably, springs from the shared sense of freedom: pure chance has brought us together; a train station will separate us. Trains let us remain passive without feeling we're lazy. As Tim Parks, the author of *Italian Ways*, has observed, the railroad frees us "from any responsibility for speed and steering." We can think, work, dream, or we can be distracted; we can even worry, if the day and the journey push us in that direction.

Trains help us think. I will admit that I envied Tishani Doshi, a talented Indian poet, for the title of a book she recently published: *Everything Begins Elsewhere*. It's true. The sources of our thoughts often lie concealed in the wrinkles of a journey. Traveling often produces a combination of imagination, stimuli, encounters, and memories. The ingredients are added and combined at the appropriate time. The railroad is the most effective blender available.

The train is a symbol of change, of movement. For the past thirty years—maybe longer—we've never stopped talking about the same old things in Italy (corruption, crime, the problems of the South, the hardened arteries of our politics, the decline of labor unions, the glacial slowness of our administration); the national narrative is stuck. We have the impression we're not progressing. That is why nations that are less well organized or poorer than Italy—India, for example, or China—tell pollsters they're happier than we are. They have the impression they're moving forward. Progress is exciting; being stuck is discouraging.

Naturally, going forward is riskier than standing still. You can't go off the rails if you're not moving. And sometimes it doesn't take much at all to derail. The very same day my editor proposed the book's title—in an incredible coincidence—a train just outside Milan actually did go off the rails: a serious accident caused by a small defective piece of track fastener, just nine inches long. It happens to us all—people and nations. We can derail because of a trifle. But it is our duty to fix the track and continue our journey, even if it's a difficult one, even if we know it won't go on forever. To discover you're resilient is a source of relief, and relief is a sophisticated form of happiness.

Literature is full of good examples. One such is *Stoner*, a novel by John Williams. It tells the story of a teacher trying to give meaning to a life full of disappointments, but a life in which he has stubbornly held his own. He did what he could. He kept going. He got back on track after derailing. At a certain point he writes: "A sense of his own identity came upon him with sudden force, and he felt the power of it. He was himself, and he knew what he had been." We all need moments like this. Sometimes heroism consists of accepting that we're not heroes, and just plugging away.

///////////////////

Trains—when they're not an obligation and a restriction—are an exercise in mental hygiene. We travel alone and we travel with others: two ideal conditions, provided you can alternate freely between them. As we roll down the rails, life comes to visit us from outside, in the form of an unexpected smile, a talkative family, two young people speaking only with their eyes.

Every train provides a narrative, included in the price of the ticket. A beginning and an end, a route as the plot. That is why trains appear so often in movies, and sometimes actually rise to the role of protagonist: think *Shanghai Express* with Marlene Dietrich and *Night Train to Lisbon* with Jeremy Irons. That's the reason so many authors have chosen to set their works on trains ("The Lost Special" by Arthur Conan Doyle, *Murder on the Orient Express* by Agatha Christie, "Jeumont, 51 Minutes Wait!" by Georges Simenon). Even if you're not planning espionage or murder, take a train. Someone—I can't remember who—wrote: "Train tracks are a closing zipper." At a time of oversharing, like the present, that's both reassuring and a consolation.

My generation loved trains. For Americans now in their fifties, the words "Eurail Pass" have the same exotic and erotic appeal as "cruise liner" for those in their seventies. Even now, there are plenty of young people who understand: trains give you an insider's view of Europe and beyond—on the cheap, if you're organized. Trains always represent the national culture. On Russian trains, there is inevitably a tea samovar; on American trains, there's eggs and bacon for breakfast; on Italian trains, there's conversation around the clock.

I'll never forget my honeymoon, on the Trans-Siberian Railroad, from Moscow to Beijing, in the summer of 1986. When my mentor, the great journalist Indro Montanelli, heard about it, he opened wide those light blue eyes of his and told me: "It's the most ridiculous idea I've ever heard in my life. Your punishment will be to write about it" (and that's exactly what happened). Later, again by train, and again with the same wife, I traveled from the Baltic to the Bosphorus during Communism's last chaotic summer (1989). In more recent years—with my wife, with our son, alone, or with Italian friends and German colleagues—I've crossed the United States from the Atlantic to the Pacific (twice, once by the southern route and once by the northern route); I've followed the train tracks from Moscow to Lisbon; I've crossed Europe vertically (from Berlin to Palermo) and Australia horizontally (Sydney–Perth, a route that includes the world's longest dead-straight stretch of railway track).

And then there is my recent European journey with Donald Trump: from Naples to London, by train, with a bobblehead version of the forty-fifth president, in the fall of 2017, one year after his election. Traveling with a statuette, let me say, has its advantages. This Donald doesn't talk, he doesn't tweet, and you don't have to ask people what they think of the forty-fifth president; they come and tell you.

But the destination isn't the main thing. All great journeys—from Catholic pilgrimages to the Grand Tour, from the first trip we take with our friends to our honeymoon—are, after all, a discovery of ourselves. And it might be with a little help from a stranger. Trains are rolling confession booths, and we're almost never close friends with our father confessor. We're looking for who we are: places and people are the mirrors that travel with us. It's not an easy thing to admit. And in fact, let's just go ahead and deny it. Still, it happens. The view we're really interested in is inside us, not out the windows, however lovely that may be.

//////////////////

The book you now hold in your hands is the product of this conviction. Travel in general—and train travel in particular—is an opportunity to think, sum up, confront ideas; but it is especially a way to understand what we're like, and what we've become. We, and the world around us. Once you turn the last page, I feel sure, you'll have understood something more about Italy, Europe, and America; and even—I hope— about yourselves.

That's what happened to me. Of them all, the most stirring journey was crossing America overland with my twenty-year-old son. From Washington, DC, to Washington State, five thousand miles by train, bus, and car. A mutual discovery, I believe. A gift that my son, Antonio, chose to bestow upon me. A story that, with his permission, I choose to tell you.

From Washington to Washington: With Antonio Across America

I haven't been carrying him at all. He's been carrying me!

ROBERT M. PIRSIG,
ZEN AND THE ART OF MOTORCYCLE MAINTENANCE

The Europeans Don't Live Here Anymore

The house is made of wood, painted white, and looks west. The front door is black, with a carved fan decoration above it, and there are three windows with the shutters nailed to the facade, on the off chance that some modest European might have the impulse to shut them at night.

But there's no danger of that now. The Europeans don't live here anymore.

In 1994 and 1995, I lived here with my wife, Ortensia, and my son, Antonio, aged two. I was the only foreign correspondent for a brand-new Italian newspaper, *La Voce*, and I was based in Washington, DC. My official title was "bureau chief," but to be honest, there was no bureau. I worked from home in Georgetown. It was a gracious part of America, full of talkative ladies and hyperactive dogs. Bill Clinton was in the White House—Monica Lewinsky, too, as it turned out—but politics was not the first topic of conversation. My neighbors talked mostly about the renovation of Volta Park and told me how to maintain tree boxes properly—they suspected that, as a newcomer, I'd be inattentive and possibly sloppy.

We left one morning in May 1995, after holding a yard sale that amused the neighbors and loading a moving truck that angered the wife of the senator from Montana. ("Move that truck! I'm married to the senator from Montana!") The truck carried away what was left of our furnishings, to be packed into a wooden crate and shipped to our house in Crema, Italy. Once it had been emptied and painted green, ventilated with a door and windows, and roofed with terra-cotta tiles, the crate went to live at the far end of the backyard, in the shade of the oak and the plane trees. A perfect playhouse.

But the two-year-old boy has now turned twenty; he'd be embarrassed to take his girlfriend into the playhouse, even if we, his parents, would find it romantic. The crate from our move back is baked by sun and drenched by rain. I tell Antonio these things, but he ignores me. He's looking at the American house where he was a toddler, amused rather than moved. "I remembered it as being bigger," he says, forgetting that back then he was smaller.

An evening in June, green leaves and blue sky: this time of year, Georgetown is at its best. We try to reenact a photograph snapped right here in 1995, on the sidewalk in front of the house: *Papà* kneeling, Antonio standing with a soccer ball in his hands. The difference is that, back then, even on my knees, I was still taller than he was; now I'm hip-high next to him. The new owners, Griff and Kathleen Jenkins, watch us with smiles on their faces. Griff busies himself with a pair of shears, enthusiastically trimming up and down the street, to make sure that no branches interfere with the Italians' photography.

We've become friends over the years. The Jenkins family—father, mother, two teenage girls—cheerfully tolerated the stream of readers who came to see the house they'd read about. To reassure visitors they had the right place, and dissuade them from ringing the doorbell, they fastened a small bronze plaque to the door, engraved with the title of the book that tells the story of our lives behind those windows: *Ciao, America!: An Italian Discovers the U.S.*

Antonio laughs. "Congratulations! I thought you had to be dead to get a bronze plaque."

The white wooden house on Thirty-fourth Street NW—a one-way street running downhill, then and now—has been renovated, but not beyond recognition. The ground floor, where we played soccer on the hardwood floors, using the fireplace as our goalpost, is still bright and sunny. The downstairs, with the kitchen and dining room, still resembles a fallout shelter: badly lit, sparsely furnished. We step out the back door into the yard. Everything looks familiar. The tree with white blossoms is where it ought to be, the magnolia still showers leaves into the neighbors' yard, and the cement cherub is still making his way through the rosebushes. It did its best—of that I feel sure—but in twenty years it still hasn't managed to become an antique. Older, perhaps, but not necessarily wiser. Much like us, much like America, which it's now time for us to go check up on. The plan is to travel from Washington, DC, to Washington State, by the southern route. By train, though not without variations. An American curve five thousand miles long, running through Atlanta, New Orleans, Dallas, Flagstaff, Tucson, San Diego, Los Angeles, and San Francisco. Destination: Seattle. A trip with my son, to discover the joy of letting him make the decisions. He always has, truth be told, but now it's official. Because there's no two ways about it: Antonio knows what he wants. For instance, here's one condition he insisted on: we have to spend at least two days in Washington, DC, at a certain hotel near Dupont Circle. Ostensibly, to recover from his transatlantic flight and jet lag. Actually, though, because he wants to eat breakfast in the room, and he knows that he can forget about that luxury on an Amtrak train.

////////////////

Washington, DC, is a green, geometric misunderstanding that brings together American and foreign tourists. Fifteen million of them every year. They arrive expecting to find a monumental, transitory, artificial city, built by politicians for politics, cut off from the rest of the country. Which is nonsense. Washington, DC, is more representative of America than New York or Los Angeles, which are both unique and irreproducible. There's only one White House, but there are lots and lots of white houses just like ours. They're as lively as they are numerous. To a fault, in some cases.

Washington is a mixed-up, fanciful city, muggy in the summer, freezing in the winter, magical in springtime, brisk in the fall. A strange city: a center of power that has very little of its own. The city is not represented in Congress, which irritates the residents, seeing that they pay taxes, like all other Americans. The license plates carry the somewhat contentious motto "Taxation without representation," a variation on the slogan of the American Revolution ("No taxation without representation"). The colonists, in the middle of the eighteenth century, were protesting the fact that they were obliged to pay taxes to London but had no say in parliamentary decisions. The residents at the turn of the twenty-first century are objecting because they are obliged to pay federal taxes, and they have no say in Congress. Washington is a border city: it's the South of the North, and the North of the South. A city where whites are in the minority, where plants grow luxuriantly, and where many houses have a porch. The classic WPA guides—a series of guidebooks to the American states, published between 1937 and 1945, under the auspices of the Federal Writers' Project—informed visitors: "Everywhere in the Capital one hears the indolent cadence of Southern speech, and encounters that admirable though often irritating Southern characteristic—the innate aversion to hurry and worry."

Well, that's not the way it is anymore. For many years now, the nation's capital has been an anxious, brusque, and formal place, like the rest of America's cities when it comes to work. Even on a day like today. The heat is ferocious, the humidity oppressive. Antonio looks at me and says nothing, but he drags his feet as if to ask, "Where on earth have you brought me?" Beneath a sky the color of dirty glass, men in ties and women in skirt suits dart back and forth like pinballs: they're trying to run up as many points as they can before vanishing into some quiet building. Ideally, with air-conditioning, something pinball machines don't have.

Driven by a combination of suffocation and civic duty, we visit the Newseum, where America tells its story as it likes to hear it: heroic and true to its values, with the occasional touch of enthusiastic madness. We walk past FBI headquarters. To decorate the temporary wooden barriers around the renovation work, they're using famous sayings of the presidents: in chronological order, playing no favorites. We climb up to Capitol Hill, we walk down to the Mall, and, exhausted, we suddenly remember what we ought to have known, since we've lived here before: in America no one goes for a stroll; they go somewhere and come back.

We hide out at Charlie Palmer's, a steak house that's popular with members of Congress. An austere place that could be mistaken for a hospital if it weren't for the color: mahogany instead of pale green. Antonio—sweat drenched, sleepy, and argumentative—wants a hamburger with fries. The uniformed headwaiter looks down his nose at him, the way a Venetian gondolier might look at a Realtor from Richmond, Virginia, as he snaps pictures on the Grand Canal. I look at the headwaiter. I explain to him that, in any tussle with the appetite of a jet-lagged twenty-year-old, he's bound to lose. He smiles and comes back with the hamburger.

We grab a taxi, we head for Dupont Circle, and we get stuck in traffic caused by the Pride Parade. The situation meets with the Somali taxi driver's disapproval, and he breaks off the intense conversation he's carrying on over his cell phone to curse the parade in an unidentifiable language. Antonio, suddenly wide-awake, starts asking me a series of difficult questions.

"Why are the streets full of half-naked people, but it's considered scandalous to show a breast on television? Do you remember that time at the Super Bowl?"

"What does Dykes on Bikes mean?"

"Why is DC Eagle wearing nothing but a black leather miniskirt?"

"Why is that priest in the march?"

And then, back at the hotel:

"Why did that guy in thermal underwear on the elevator offer us free condoms, but I'm still not old enough to order a beer?"

Coward that I am, I suggest he ask the coffee shop waitress, who looks to be about his age; but Antonio, lying in his turn, claims that his English isn't up to the task. But the young woman is talkative. She tells us that the Gay Pride Parade snarls traffic and brings in plenty of customers; her salary basically goes to pay taxes, seven hundred dollars every two weeks. She makes her money off tips. With foreigners, it's best to be direct, she tells us; they don't always know it's customary to leave a tip, and if the tip is generous, all the better. She doesn't seem particularly interested in the world around her, nor do the Americans in the restaurant seem particularly interested in her.

We leave, go into Kramerbooks to buy a Rand McNally road atlas, then walk down Sixteenth Street—the street that once separated the world of the whites from everyone else—to Pennsylvania Avenue. Outdoor café tables, bicycles leaning against walls, people chatting. Washington, DC, seems to have figured out what it had forgotten twenty years ago: there's no law against slowing down, no regulation forbidding you to stop and chat with your friends on the street.

///////////////

Union Station has changed since 1995. The American love of strict procedure hasn't, though. We all have to wait in one place; we all have to enter the gate at the same time, then wait our turn to be taken to the faraway track in an electric vehicle. The driver, dressed in a scarlet uniform—age impossible to guess, and with an inexplicable enthusiasm—drives and shouts as if he were competing in a rodeo. He drops us off at Track J25, train no. 19, destination New Orleans. He wishes us happy travels, eager to reprise his show for the next passengers. We take possession of our compartment, which is a concentrate of American mechanical fantasies: a sink that folds away and becomes a step, for instance. We need to find a place to put everything. We'll be spending a little more than twenty-four hours in this compartment, but we can't spend that time with the wheels of our roller suitcases on our necks. I show Antonio my copy of *Travels with Charley*, by John Steinbeck, which I brought with me from Italy. I open the book, find the page, and read aloud:

> When I laid the ground plan of my journey, there were definite questions to which I wanted matching answers. It didn't seem to me that they were impossible questions. I suppose they could all be lumped into the single question: "What are Americans like today?"

Antonio replies: "Well, they're shorter than we are, that's for sure. At least, the ones who travel by train must be, because I'm too tall to fit in this bunk."

"Any other comments?" I ask.

He looks at the cover of the book. "Your author traveled with a dog, who barked or wagged his tail to make himself understood. I am your son, and I'd like to inform you that you're sitting on my backpack."

I have a suspicion that the boy's not going to read the book, but he's already commented on it. When he grows up, he could be a book critic. Time to go.

Night Train for New Orleans

Our train is called the Crescent, and it left Manhattan's Penn Station at 2:15 in the afternoon. It stopped, ninety-one miles later, in Philadelphia; it pulled out again at 3:55. Ninety-four miles later it arrived in Baltimore, which it left at 5:14 p.m. After forty miles it pulled into

Union Station in Washington, DC, and left again at 6:30, with two Italians aboard. An older one, euphoric. And a younger one, puzzled.

The train is supposed to reach Charlotte, North Carolina, tonight at 2:20 a.m. Atlanta, Georgia, tomorrow morning at 8:13. Birmingham, Alabama, at 10:23. And then, finally, New Orleans. Arrival scheduled at 7:32 p.m., 1,377 miles from its starting point. I'm certain of the schedules and the distances because Amtrak has salted the train cars with brochures providing all this information about the trip. The national love of numbers has been satisfied; the love of comfort— another national commandment—a little less so. Amtrak represents the side of America that is practical and unshowy; not the highly efficient, innovative, and aesthetically impeccable America. The only thing our train has in common with an Apple product is the color: the gleaming silver that is reminiscent of Airstream trailers and diner counters. These are places where the nation likes to see its reflection, and remember the way things were. There are three Scenic Highlights touted to the passengers:

vibrant Northeast cityscapes (that is, the train is going to run through the ramshackle outskirts of several large cities)

Blue Ridge foothills (the train won't go up into the mountains, but you'll be able to see the mountains from the windows)

Louisiana bayou country (the train is going to run through the swamplands of Louisiana)

Considering the violent downpour now under way, and the others that the weatherman is calling for, the bayou country will just be the wettest part of a very wet journey. Still—Antonio says—no train has ever been involved in a shipwreck, so there's no cause for concern.

The ticket states: "Car 1911/Room 008." "Car," to an Italian, is just one of the oddities of American English, meaning what in Italian would be *carrozza* (which is much closer to the word that would be used in Great Britain, "carriage"). "Room," in this case, is what we Italians would call a *cuccetta*, or berth. To call it a room, in fact, would seem to be overstating the case. It's a meter wide, two meters in length: maybe twenty-two square feet. The lower seats recline to form the lower bunk; the top bunk swings down from the wall. But Antonio doesn't complain: he immediately claims the lower bunk, on account of a case of alleged vertigo he doesn't actually have, and starts fiddling with his iPhone.

I tell him, from above: "Look at America out there."

He answers, from below: "Where are we going?"

Swelling with pride, I start my explanation: the Southern states, segregation, civil rights, jazz, the revolution brought by air-conditioning. He listens in rapt silence. A little too silent. I lean over: he's asleep.

The Crescent rolls on through the rain—slowly, but with admirable determination. Four matronly women in their seventies, in the adjoining berths, laugh happily, regaling one another across the corridor with tales of their adventures.

///////////////////

We show up late for breakfast, which is being served in the dining car. But the waitress, friendly and imposing, forgives me: "What would you like, honey?" At first I think she's asking me "Which do you prefer: honey or jam?" When I realize that she's *calling* me honey, I decide I like the winning enthusiasm of the old-school American waitress. The newer recruits to the profession are, often, just as well-mannered. But for them, the job is just a stop along the way to something better, and there is something automatic to their courtesy. If *they* ask, "What would you like, honey?" they really do want to know: What'll it be, honey or jam? The menu, the front of which features a romantic depiction of our train (crescent moon, trees, mountain silhouettes), offers Scrambled Eggs (548 calories), $7.50; Continental Breakfast (699 calories), $8.75;

Classic Railroad French Toast (438 calories), $9.50; Chef's Good
Morning Special (1,085 calories), $10.75; Omelet Selection (551 calo-
ries), $11.25. In italics, the traveler is warned that "occasionally, verbal
substitutions may be offered instead of printed menu selections." That's
fine: it'll just be another opportunity to talk to the waitress, and have
her call me *honey*!

//////////////////

American long-distance trains are remarkable. This is no commuter
train, like the one that runs up the Northeast coast, linking Washington, DC; Baltimore; Philadelphia; New York; and Boston. That Amtrak
train probably even has Wi-Fi, I'd bet. This one, creaking through
Georgia under a gunmetal gray sky, only has air-conditioning. Fingers
crossed that the air-conditioning works, at least.

In the U.S., only certain categories of people take the train. People
who live too far from an airport. People who are afraid of flying. People
who are young and restless. People who are old and restful. People who
have the kind of physical disabilities that airlines don't much care for:
obesity, for example. The lounge car—dark blue and white, Formica
tables, seats in Naugahyde upholstery—is a likable congregation of special cases. We're sitting with an elderly couple who boarded the train
at Greenville, South Carolina. She tells us that the station in Atlanta is
the unfriendliest one of all ("Only one elevator, just think of that!"). All
around us are solitary travelers with a book, students with a tablet,
young girls with earbuds. Antonio has pulled the hood of his sweatshirt
over his head and has joined the well-known international sect: its
members, instead of telling those around them, "Leave me alone," pull
the hoods of their sweatshirts over their heads. A toddler comes down
the aisle, festooned with pigtails and necklaces, dragging a pink teddy
bear. In a few years she, too, at nine in the morning, will pull the hood
of her sweatshirt over her head. But for now, she smiles.

It dawns on me that we are the only genuine tourists: the passengers on this train don't look like they're on vacation. In Georgia we pass through a litany of suburbs, the exponentially expanding periphery, an urban ectoplasm with a variety of names—*sprawl, exurbia, suburban supernova*—and numerous consequences. I was here for work, a few years ago. A town just north of Atlanta in Fulton County. I remember the name of the place: Alpharetta. Not even the screenwriters on *Star Trek*, after four vodka and tonics, could have come up with a name like that. One of the epicenters of the American real estate meltdown. Lots of people bought houses here on subprime mortgages; there were foreclosures here by the thousands; the banks sold house after house they had repossessed. The traces of that destructive financial hurricane can still be seen. Just try counting the FOR SALE signs.

After Atlanta, as we head west, the tempest becomes a meteorological one: no longer money blowing in the wind, this time raindrops hitting the glass. An American rainstorm, robust and methodical. The auto dealerships, full of pickup trucks and shiny banners, seem to have landed on the wrong planet. At the level crossings, we can glimpse shadows behind the windshield wipers. As we roll along the tracks running between the houses, we see backyards, bicycles, and sheds to store the toys of the children, already grown. An America caught from behind. The back of an Edward Hopper painting, rain-streaked.

///////////////////

Tallapoosa, Georgia. Tuscaloosa, Alabama. Then, a sign: CLINTON. This isn't a presidential reference. It's just one of the twenty-six places in America with that name. I explain to Antonio: Clinton is the second-most popular place-name in the U.S. after Springfield (forty-one), but leading Madison (twenty-five), Franklin (twenty-four), Washington (twenty-four), Chester (twenty-three), Marion (twenty-three), Greenville (twenty-two), Georgetown (twenty-one), and Salem (twenty-one). Then I think to myself: there was a time when you could impress your children with this kind of knowledge. These days, though, your children know that there's such a thing as Google. Two young people, a young man and a young woman, are talking at the table next to ours. Apparel: pajama pants (checkered flannel), extra-large sweatshirts, knit caps, unlaced shoes.

> **SHE:** How do you like Philly?
> **HE:** I don't.
> **SHE:** How long have you been there?
> **HE:** Three weeks.
> **SHE:** Why?
> **HE:** I moved over there with my girlfriend.
> **SHE:** What don't you like about Philly?
> **HE:** The city, I'd say.

In Alabama, intense greenery, ninety degrees; the rain has stopped, but there's still water everywhere. The train stops at Birmingham. We pass through underbrush: there is no land in sight on either side of the train; it seems to be running through a swamp. Though maybe "running" isn't the verb I should be using: we're moving at a crawl. I remind Antonio of the musical polemic between Neil Young and Lynyrd Skynyrd. Neil Young recorded the song "Alabama," accusing the state of racism ("Alabama, you got the weight on your shoulders / That's breaking your back"). The band replied with "Sweet Home Alabama" ("Well, I hope Neil Young will remember / A Southern man don't need him around anyhow"). All arguing aside, I tell him, two magnificent songs. In Meridian, Mississippi, ninety-one degrees Fahrenheit. We were scheduled to get there at noon, but we're running late. Three teenagers are traveling with their parents; they're passing through New Orleans, and they'll continue through Austin, Texas, and on to the Grand Canyon, in Arizona. The youngest is using Siri to dictate on his iPhone. He thinks he's in Montana.

At a stop, Antonio gets off the train to stretch his legs and comes close to being left on the platform, but the maternal shouts of the female train conductors foil him in that attempt.

The train starts up again. I close my computer and I open one of my favorite railway books: Paul Theroux's *The Old Patagonian Express* (after all, it's about trains, and it's about America, or the Americas). "Half of jazz is railway music, and the motion and noise of the train itself has the rhythm of jazz. This is not surprising," the author explains. "The Jazz Age was also the Railway Age. Musicians traveled by train or not at all, and the pumping tempo and the clickety-clack and the lonesome whistle crept into the songs."

Travelers are romantics. Lulled by the railroad car, I wonder, will I find all this in New Orleans?

///////////////

The best summary can be found in the Lonely Planet guide: "It's one of the tackiest experiences in the world." The heart of the French Quarter, where we recklessly made our hotel reservations, reeks of last night's liquor, hot garbage, and water left over from the street-cleaning trucks. Tourist-trap hotels alternate with cheap restaurants, clubs promise music and fun, and brass trumpets and shapely legs loom large on the neon signs, now dark. The humorist Dave Barry wrote: "The rest of the city is even looser, especially the French Quarter, which is so decadent that if the Reverend Jerry Falwell were to merely walk down the length of Bourbon Street, he would emerge at the other end with an overpowering desire to purchase leather underwear." The next morning, we board a Gray Line bus for a guided tour of the city. I'm determined to show my son that New Orleans is more than just the French Quarter. It's a dynamic city that has successfully rebounded from Hurricane Katrina (2005) and is now attracting young people from all across America.

This morning, though, all we see is retirees. They're wearing shorts, sensible shoes, and souvenir T-shirts from their hometowns (Chicago Bulls, St. Louis Cardinals), from previous trips (Yosemite National Park, SeaWorld San Diego), or announcing their overriding passions (Miller Lite, Bud Ice, Playboy). I list for my son the names of movies made in New Orleans: *Pretty Baby, The Pelican Brief, The Big Easy, The Curious Case of Benjamin Button*. And, of course, *Easy Rider*. Wyatt (Peter Fonda) and Billy (Dennis Hopper)—I explain as the seniors' bus tour pulls into St. Louis Cemetery—roll into town, wade into the Mardi Gras celebrations, visit a brothel, wander off with two prostitutes, and wind up in the Catholic cemetery, drop acid, take off their clothes, and grapple with the naked girls and the statues. Since then, no other film crew has been authorized to shoot in this cemetery. "Why am I not surprised?" Antonio asks wryly.

In the afternoon, we board the steamboat *Natchez*. "A truly classic expression of the best of America's great steamboat tradition," says a sign. We choose the Harbor Jazz Cruise on the Mississippi. The big red stern wheel starts turning and pushes us through the tobacco-brown water: as we stand watching it, everyone else gets all the best seats. After a twenty-minute ride along the river, we reach the Domino sugar refinery, reverse course, and then it's time for lunch. Red beans and rice! Coleslaw! Bread pudding! Fried fish! The passengers seem to come back to life. A jazz combo plays "When the Saints Go Marching In" and sells CDs. The bartender, originally from Brooklyn, figures out that we're Italians and tells us that he once worked for Lidia Bastianich. Why are we standing in the Texas Bar, on a Louisiana steamboat, talking to a guy from New York? Antonio asks me. Because it's the only place with air-conditioning, I explain.

This evening, the Garden District awaits us, luxuriant with magnolias and flowers, where New Orleans, the heart of the South, approaches the European fantasy. Tomorrow morning, what awaits us is a bus to Dallas, where those fantasies will be rapidly dismantled.

Greyhound to Dallas

Traveling with your children is complicated and literary; and it's literary because it's complicated. American authors have a certain tradition when it comes to the subject. Robert M. Pirsig takes Chris, eleven years old, on the back of his motorcycle (*Zen and the Art of Motorcycle Maintenance*). The protagonist of Cormac McCarthy's *The Road* takes his boy out into an apocalyptic America. And, as we've seen, John Steinbeck takes his dog with him, for lack of willing offspring (*Travels with Charley*).

Almost invariably the children (and the pets) wind up being the audience: Papa thinks it over, decides, and announces; the rest of the family listens and obeys. Our children, in books and outside them, are at risk of becoming our walking audience. And summer is the perfect time to put on the performance. Have you ever wondered why my generation, in our sixties childhoods, played games that involved spotting license plates and car colors? And why the kids of today dive into their tablets and video games? The reason remains the same. It's so they don't have to listen to their parents' monologues while on vacation, after being forced to do it all year long.

Therefore, the first rule of traveling with Antonio is this: limit the chatter. Silence, between two people who know each other well, can be a symptom of malaise—or solid proof that they understand each other without saying a word. I have no doubt about it. When he and I travel together, we don't talk much, because there's no need to talk much. He knows, I know, and we know. We know that sometimes I listen without hearing, while he doesn't listen but—I can't say how—always hears everything. We know that we both overdo it with our iPhones, for different reasons: I use mine for work; he uses his for play. Whereupon Antonio retorts: "Your work is fun for you, so it's as if you were playing, so quit griping."

Four years ago, when Antonio was sixteen, we rode along the coasts of Sardinia on a pair of motorcycles. Days at the beach can be lovely even when the cold mistral wind is blowing out of the northwest, and we're waiting for a summer that refuses to come: the morning at the water's edge, with red flags warning us to stay out of the water and beached jellyfish on the sand; the evening in front of the television set, watching a rerun of a soccer match. You look out the window, you admire the holm oaks and juniper trees defying the wind, and you think to yourself: I remember when I was here at his age, and everything seemed shiny and new, and the motorcycles were parked out front like horses tied up outside a saloon, and we ate too much bad food between meals, and the girls from Belgium had the nicest laughs. Now it's their turn, our kids' turn, and every so often they'll let us watch them as they head out into open water, new sailboats heading out of port. There is nothing we're supposed to do. Just wave, with one hand, careful not to let anyone else see.

The great challenge in travel is not arriving at the glamorous foreign city, but solving the departure problem, finding a way out of it, without flying. Buses are usually nasty, and bus stations the world over are dens of thieves, cutpurses, intimidators, mountebanks and muggers.

With these reassuring words by Paul Theroux in my mind, we leave the hotel to catch our bus for Dallas at the Greyhound station. The important thing, I explain to Antonio, is to get there on time. "Well, let's not overdo it," he says.

We overdid it. The only people besides us at the bus station are a couple of security guards just getting off their shift. Shops are shuttered, benches and seats empty. To make up for it, I point out that the station is lit up like broad daylight. "That might be because it's daytime," points out my son, who chooses the least useful moments to emerge from his generation's morning lethargy.

And in fact, it is daytime. And we're here *very* early. We came by cab, and the driver had a heartbreaking jazz dirge on the radio and the air-conditioning turned down to sixty degrees: cool enough for a couple of corpses in summertime, but not suited to a couple of Italian tourists showing up early for a bus. In America, air-conditioning in summer, like central heating in winter, is brutal. The equivalent devices in Italy may show a certain restraint, as if they are embarrassed to alter the pattern of the seasons, but American air-conditioning systems are unashamedly efficient. Not only here in the South; everywhere. "Hot" here does not mean "tepid." It means "searing." And "cold" has nothing to do with merely "cool." We're talking "arctic." Americans who go into a waiting room or an office, a theater or a museum, are looking for a violent shock, not a caress. An extreme experience. The worst are supermarkets, where the goose bumps on the customers provide an attractive complement to those on sale in the poultry section. But criticism is an expression of interest. Air-conditioning is, for Europeans, at least, an obsession, a favorite theme of conversation at dinner parties . . . and on trains, of course. In fact, I am sure people actually avoid sitting next to me so as not to be subjected to my complaints about air-conditioning.

////////////////////

It's two hours before the bus leaves for Dallas. The ticket counter isn't open yet. Waiting with us is a couple who certainly has a right to the senior discount. He is wearing a pair of pink overalls, and he looks like he just stepped out of a Norman Rockwell illustration; she's loaded down with packages, her hair needs fixing, and she has lots of things to say. None of them especially agreeable, to judge from the look on his face.

Evelyn Waugh wrote: "One does not travel, any more than one falls in love, to collect material. It is simply part of one's life." That's true, but there's certainly a great deal of material here. The America of long-distance bus travel is an assortment of astonishment, somnolence, and displeasures united by a condition that is basically humiliating: that of not owning a car. No car-owning American would shut himself up in a

Greyhound for twelve hours, crossing Louisiana, from southeast to northwest, and Texas. Antonio looks at me: *Then why are we?*

///////////////

The silvery bus—greyhound on the side, tinted windows—finally leaves the station, practically full. On board, there's a Wi-Fi signal and the smell of toilets, and it's not possible to choose between the two. In Baton Rouge, just eighty miles away, a five-minute stop is announced, which turns into a forty-five minute layover. No one, except for yours truly, asks for an explanation.

In the Baton Rouge station, we get a cup of coffee in the shop-with-tables run by an Indian from Gujarat. He sells practically everything. Coca-Cola, Mountain Dew, Trident chewing gum, Benadryl, Advil, and aspirin in single-dose packets, maps, cookies, padlocks, razors, nail clippers, earbuds: the full spectrum of American on-the-road self-sufficiency. We get back aboard and the bus pulls out.

Grand Cane, Grosse Tete—the place-names in Louisiana are quite curious.

We continue north. After Lafayette, Opelousas and Alexandria lie before us.

The Greyhound rolls on; Antonio plays; I observe: inside, more than outside. A mother and son: she can't be thirty yet; he's already a teenager. A husband and wife: they never speak, just stare straight ahead. And then there are aged hippies, bewildered youngsters, unspeaking giants. In the seat ahead of us is a pregnant young girl, with two sons beside her. She has small tattoos on her face, and a larger one on her neckline: *Fast Money*. Something that, evidently, never showed up.

A guy with red hair and a high blood-alcohol reading tries to pick up our seat neighbor, a woman in her early forties of Italian descent, from Savannah, Georgia. "I'm running a day late," she explains to me. "I love my husband," she tells her drunken suitor. In his disappointment, he pulls out his cell phone and starts calling everyone he knows.

He practically shouts into the phone when someone finally picks up: "What a crappy thing! I woke up sitting next to the biggest asshole on the bus!" Since English, unlike Italian, doesn't specify gender in these cases, the woman and I exchange a glance, trying to figure out which of us is the recipient of the compliment.

The Greyhound rolls on. By afternoon, the faces are starting to look familiar. Small instances of courtesy toward other passengers begin to spring up. In Shreveport, we get stuck waiting for our connection to Dallas, which is running an hour late. A young woman in the waiting room is reading *The New Yorker*; it's incongruous, to say the least. Why did she choose to take the bus? I ask her. "It's cheap," she replies without bothering to look up.

A colossus carrying a skateboard comes over, clearly upset: "Hey you! You aren't eating my potato chips, are you?" No, why? "Well, you know how it is, people are ruthless around bus stations," he says, justifying his assumption. Then he notices Antonio's majestic Maori tattoo, from ankle to knee. That's what my son brought back from a recent trip to Australia, instead of a bottle of Vegemite. He leans over, observes it closely, studies it. "That's . . . awesome! Man! Where the fuck you do that?" Language aside, I understand that the colossus is impressed. I tell Antonio, in Italian, to take charge of the public relations job.

I look at him. Smiling and nonchalant, he's the center of attention. He's chatting with two matronly women, low necklines and buxom; two young people who started out from Jackson, Mississippi; a skinny guy in an XXL T-shirt, with tattooed eyebrows. A young man dressed in a basketball uniform looks up from his copy of *The 21 Most Effective Prayers of the Bible* and joins the knot of admirers oohing and aahing over the tattoo. It's a chorus of *Give me five!* and compliments for the young European traveler. Even his elderly traveling companion takes on a degree of interest in the eyes of the other travelers. "The sexiest calf in Texas!" a young blond woman whispers to me, as she combs her wet hair. No doubt about it, I tell her. Never mind that we're in Louisiana.

At last, we pull out. There're still three hours and 188 miles to go along I-20 West. We enter Texas at last: we're going to pass through Marshall, Longview, Tyler, and Mesquite. A Latino couple, arms wrapped around each other under a single blanket, show no signs of being in a hurry. "By the grace of God, we'll get there!" the reader of biblical prayers declares enthusiastically.

There is Dallas, and it announces its existence with a lake of lights in the distance. A young Mexican boy, in the seat in front of us, explains in an undertone that he's going back to see his grandmother. At the bus station exit, there's a guy waiting for him with a souped-up car, stereo blasting. The little boy waves good-bye to us from the car window, and then vanishes into the heat and darkness.

A Toyota Across the West

Renting a car in Texas is easy. All you need is a credit card, a driver's license, and the ability to speak Spanish. The people behind the counter don't always seem to have a full mastery of the English language.

The car is a Toyota RAV4, black. We pick it up in downtown Dallas, and we'll drop it off in front of a hotel in San Diego, California. The price, because we made our reservations well in advance, is trifling. But it lacks a GPS navigator, and Antonio insists we need to buy one. We find a Best Buy, where I stand openmouthed before the miles of aisles of monumental refrigerators. "They're too big, no way they'll fit in the car," says the designated driver, a practical-minded young man. We buy a TomTom for eighty dollars and leave.

Guided by a small, piping, authoritarian voice, we decide to explore the city before heading west. We visit the site of the assassination of John F. Kennedy, on November 22, 1963, though we decide to politely decline the offer to take the "JFK Assassination Tour"; we also avoid the guided tour of the Southfork Ranch, the television home of J. R.

(on *Dallas*); we do, however, enter the museum of nature and science named after Ross Perot; we also gaze at the stiletto heels and miniskirts on McKinney Avenue. The *Dallas Morning News* informs us that Governor Rick Perry is proposing that truancy become a criminal offense.

It's always nice to get back to Texas.

From Dallas to San Diego is 1,184 miles as the crow flies, or 1,363 miles (2,193 kilometers) by road. But we have a number of detours planned along the way.

We drive through Irving and Fort Worth, heading for Abilene. The radio keeps playing a song by George Strait called "Run." We like it. I remember when I was Antonio's age and I drove through these parts packed into a motor home with five friends. It was 1977, Jimmy Carter had just entered the White House, and Elvis Presley was going to meet his maker. There were two big songs that summer, both by Fleetwood Mac: "Don't Stop" and "Dreams." The first helped to pump us up; the second helped us to dream about girls. Both are things that have come easily to twenty-year-olds throughout history.

As we head west—my boy is driving, one way of tearing him away from his iPhone—I realize that the choice of radio stations is quite limited: stations that play music, stations that preach, and not much else. I pick the ones playing music, and I start to notice how repetitive the music and lyrics are. By combining the following expressions, I announce, we, too, could become songwriters around here. In alphabetical order:

baby trust me

best friend

blue sky

desert highway

just close your eyes

out of town

pickup truck

stand by me

The TomTom cheerfully informs us: "Follow I-20 for four hundred fourteen miles." I translate mentally into European distances: 666 kilometers, which is almost always long enough to take you out of any given country. Here, that doesn't even take us out of the state of Texas.

//////////////////

The American interstate system is a fair representation of the national mentality: it's a logical system. An even number, say I-20, runs east–west (the numbering rises from south to north: our I-20, as I look at the map, lies above the I-10 and below the I-40). An odd number (I-35), on the other hand, indicates a north–south route. If it's a triple-digit number, and the first digit is odd, then the route leaves the highway, never to intersect again (520). If it's a triple-digit number and the first digit's even, then the route runs to the city or around it and then back out to the highway (820). "It's interesting. Just think about it," I suggest to the driver. "Do I have to?" he replies.

Antonio speaks without taking his eyes off the road. A wise choice, because the way people drive here is different from what we're used to in Italy. There is a level of predictability that you're not allowed to buck. The highways are already convoys, even before driverless cars are officially introduced: everyone goes one behind the other, no one jumps ahead, and above all, you need to get into the right lane in plenty of time! If you're looking to irritate American drivers—in big cities or on long stretches of highway—then just cut across lanes without warning to take an exit. Yielding is considered a form of weakness. Interfering with your attempt to merge: righteous retribution.

That said, I like American roads, especially here in the West: blame it on the movies. At every stopover you can upload (food, drinks, gasoline) and download (restrooms, trash). Every semitrailer and big rig—shiny, accessorized, lit up—is a display of pride. Every advertising sign is an expression of commercial enthusiasm. *The Best Seafood Combo! The Greatest Family Lodging!* The obsession with being the best/the greatest is everywhere and is fascinating. A simple study of the comparatives would prove that they can't *all* be the best; some of them must necessarily be worse than the others. But such details do nothing to discourage the nation's entrepreneurial passions, and that's something to be admired.

At Cisco two cars being towed swerve back and forth. A religious radio station informs us: "We don't quote from best sellers unless they're edifying." A service station posts the announcement: "Anyone entering with an unregistered firearm may face a fine not greater than $10,000." In Clyde, Texas, the Whataburger (*Proudly owned and operated since 1950*) offers apple pie for ninety-nine cents. The girl serving us is named Autumn. Three kitchen workers, dressed in orange like convicts, are out back, smoking cigarettes. On the window is written: "One nation under God, indivisible." The first curve in the road appears at 3:55 in the afternoon, around exit 233. At 5 p.m. the thermometer rises above ninety degrees Fahrenheit (thirty-two degrees Celsius) for the first time. We pass Odessa (exit 116), a city of oil and business, especially business having to do with oil. It's mentioned in James A. Michener's *Texas* as the town where "you are more likely to be murdered . . . than in any other city in the nation." The book was written in 1985; let's hope things have changed since then. A sign announces: RABBIT RODEO! Would that be a rodeo with rabbits instead of bulls and horses? Not exactly: the competitors try to lasso jackrabbits. Or make that "tried to"; the practice of rabbit rodeos, first introduced in 1932, was discontinued after 1978 due to the objections of the ASPCA. All that remains is a statue: an enormous jackrabbit, ears in the wind, at the corner of West Eighth Street and North Sam Houston Avenue.

We stop at another service station. They sell denim shirts for $14.99, Sue Grafton audiobooks, energy drinks in giant phosphorescent bottles, Klondike ice cream bars, and beef jerky—a kind of meat chewing gum. We buy some, but I can't talk Antonio into trying it. It's going to lie in the caddy between the front seats for the rest of the trip, silently chiding us.

I start to realize that we're drawn to gas stations. We spend more time in them than we strictly need to. Maybe it's because we like feeling part of a mechanism that allows the United States to satisfy its hunger for forward movement and procure its basic necessities: restroom, gas, sodas, cookies, and then go. In effect, all basic human needs are available at a service station: drink (refrigerators from outer space, lit up like rocket ships), food (potato chips, hot dogs, hamburgers), bathroom break and washing up (immense, austere, and functional restrooms), information (maps, newspapers), relaxation (music CDs, audiobooks), excitement (magazines featuring young women endowed with colossal front bumpers; if they were to get into a head-on collision with a semitrailer, they'd get the best of it). Usually, there's a motel not far away: sleep, too, then.

Our motel is at Pecos, population eight thousand, best known for growing cantaloupes and for having been the site, on July 4, 1883, of the first rodeo in history (at least, so they claim). Pecos is one of the many West Texas towns founded during the construction of the Texas and Pacific Railway. The motel is called the Swiss Chalet, not a name that you'd expect on the eastern edge of the Chihuahuan Desert. The reason is explained at the motel entrance, with an abundance of documentation: Hansueli Schlunegger, with his wife, Annamarie, arrived here from Switzerland in 1959 and built the place.

The Swiss love of tidiness, along with the Texan passion for tradition, has produced a sort of übermotel—a concentrate of predictability and reassurance that we find touching. *Consistency!* shouts our motel room the instant we open the door.

Inside we find:

a bed the size of a Manhattan studio apartment

a television set only a little smaller than the bed

a spacious worktable

a kettle to heat water for instant coffee (and packets of same)

a reading chair (Bible to go with it)

camo-pattern wall-to-wall carpeting (a stain just becomes part of the decor)

a bathroom without sharp edges or corners (hurting yourself would be a challenge)

a single-handle shower (easy to adjust with shampoo in your eyes)

conveniently located electrical outlets (no need to slither across the carpet to reach them)

lamps with switches on the base (easy to find in the dark)

uncluttered countertops (no bric-a-brac, no tourist brochures)

simplified, antiseptically clean remote control

Outside (*You can enjoy the patio!*): a small metal table with a central recess for bottles, ensuring they won't fall and break. In the corners, three trash cans eager to be of assistance. Sorry, fellows: we have nothing to discard, not even our fixations with America.

//////////////

There's one sure way to complicate your life: fill it with expectations. It happens at work, in friendships, in love, in families. There are people who place great expectations on their sports teams, singers, actors, even politicians. When those expectations are disappointed, we are crushed. That's the emblematic experience of these years we live in: short-lived dreams and long faces. Certainly, we have to make some emotional investments. A person without expectations is robotic. But a person with too many expectations is reckless.

Travel and vacations also ride on expectations. Friends, love affairs, relatives, traveling companions, destinations: everything needs to be exciting and gratifying. But the burden of expectations that we constantly place on relationships and places can be insidious. Expectations become demands. We build a mental film—be it documentary, romantic comedy, animated cartoon (it depends)—and then we're disappointed if the reality turns out to be a minor horror flick.

For instance, I had high expectations of El Paso, a city on the Mexican border, along the banks of the Rio Grande. It's a literary and cinematic destination, like Casablanca or Samarkand. When Antonio asked me, "Why do we need to go there?" I looked at him aghast: *El Paso, don't you see?* As if the name alone were enough. El Paso! In my imagination, I pictured it as exotic, silent, seething, sharp shadows and implacable sunshine.

As far as the sunshine was concerned, it was exactly as I'd expected. We got there and the GPS navigator went on a heat strike: too hot, it announced. It's Sunday, early afternoon: the streets are empty; the shops are shuttered. American advertising in Spanish, dusty cars. A sign says: BUY AMERICAN SAVE JOBS! We look for a place to eat lunch, and we find it. I ask how long it would take to cross the river into Mexico and have a quick look around Ciudad Juárez. Matthew, a student waiter at Crave Kitchen & Bar, says: "Don't do it."

"When I was in high school, it was normal to go to Juárez. Not anymore. You never know what might happen, especially at night. Things are okay here, I guess. Nothing exciting. El Paso is always on the edge of crappiness."

But Ciudad Juárez has passed that boundary and ventured well beyond. A few years ago, it was ranked as the most dangerous city on the planet, with more than sixty murders a week, with a population of 1.5 million. Many of the victims have been young women. Dark-haired, small, poor women, who worked in the *maquiladoras*, factories that assemble products to export to the U.S. These women were found outside the city, raped, mutilated, and murdered. There are various theories on the phenomenon. The most horrible one is also the most likely: they are considered disposable human beings. And here, when you dispose of something, you dump it in the desert.

Now Ciudad Juárez's murder rate has dropped to ten a week, but the Mexican narcos consider it—along with Tijuana, just south of San Diego—to be their business headquarters, and they fight for control of the place with utter ferocity. This year, the Rio Grande Valley has become the chief entryway for illegal immigration into the United States, taking supremacy away from Tucson, Arizona, after twenty years.

In the hopes of joining the more than eleven million Mexican-born immigrants already in the United States, migrants are willing to face the desert, the rattlesnakes, the gangs of murderers, seven hundred miles of barbed wire fence, and La Migra (as they call the border police). In 2012 there were about 360,000 arrests—the American authorities call them, euphemistically, apprehensions—compared to the roughly 1.6 million in 2000. Human traffickers cross the river on jury-rigged rafts, or else they enter American territory and unceremoniously dump dozens of people in the open desert. Many of them come from Guatemala, Honduras, or El Salvador. "They cross the border fearlessly," we are told. Just a few days ago, at La Joya, a small town on the Rio Grande, a single border guard tried to stop twenty people: they took one look at him and scattered in twenty different directions.

We nod our heads, we look at the river, and we resume driving west. Immediately after we cross the New Mexico state line, we're stopped at a roadblock by police checking for illegals. The officers quickly check our Italian passports, and hand them back with a smile. Then they notice the Maori tattoo on Antonio's leg. The smiles fade and they ask him to get out of the vehicle. I'm tempted to tell them, "Hey, that tattoo met with tremendous admiration at a bus station in Louisiana!" But I keep silent. They let us go. At seven that night we retire to our room in the Best Western in Lordsburg, New Mexico, to watch game five of the NBA championship. Outside, heat and copper mines. Inside, hamburgers, beers, and air-conditioning. It's just us three: son, father, and America, with no one else to disturb us.

//////////////////////

There's no cell phone reception, so no Google Maps. I'm delighted, and delegate to Antonio the task of finding our way to Cochise County on the Rand McNally road atlas. I hope he finds it, because this place isn't exactly packed with people.

Small dust storms move across the landscape, and the sun beats down on the rocks. It's brutally hot. A scorched land where men and animals come out at night, in search of relief. The animal dens are invisible. The dens of the people are marked by beat-up mailboxes, threatening signs (NO TRESPASSING! KEEP OUT!), wandering paths heading toward provisional-looking houses and cluttered yards: car parts, metal and wood, empty barrels, and discarded appliances.

This is an America that is still white. While Latinos may constitute forty percent of the population in Tucson, there are none to be seen here. A hyperrealistic America that Europeans glimpse in passing in a movie or a novel, only to dismiss it. It's too different: we prefer the multicultural cities with their malls, restaurants, and commercial smiles. "What can I do for you, sir?" is something you're unlikely to hear in the gas stations around Gleeson, Arizona.

For tourists, the destinations are many. Tombstone, for instance. Twice a day, they reenact the Gunfight at the O.K. Corral (October 26,

1881), made famous by books and movies. The chief lawman for the city, Deputy U.S. Marshal Virgil Earp, backed by his brothers Wyatt and Morgan Earp and their friend Doc Holliday, intended to disarm Tom McLaury, Frank McLaury, Ike Clanton, and Billy Clanton. Thirty gunshots later, three outlaws were dead. Virgil and Morgan Earp were seriously wounded; Doc Holliday was shot in the hip. Only Wyatt Earp emerged unhurt. In the reenactment we witnessed, the part of Billy Clanton was played by a well-mannered young man named Jim Robèrt. "Pronounced like the French," he specified. When he's not falling down dead in front of tourists, he's a luthier. While he dusts himself off, we talk about Cremona, the center of Italian violin making.

///////////////////

As I look out at the wings lined up in the scorching hot Arizona desert, and my son tells me to stop complaining, I wonder: Why do Americans love planes so passionately? Fine movies (*Dr. Strangelove, Top Gun*), excellent books (Don DeLillo's *Underworld, The World According to Garp* by John Irving), good music (Jefferson Airplane). A nation in love with takeoffs and landings. We Italians prefer to go for walks.

The place is called the Pima Air & Space Museum, on the outskirts of Tucson. Part of the museum is indoors, and part is outdoors, which gives you an opportunity to wander around in one of the weirdest places on the planet: the Aerospace Maintenance and Regeneration Group (AMARG) at Davis-Monthan Air Force Base. It's a parking lot for 4,400 airplanes, worth a combined thirty-five billion dollars. That's 8,800 wings waiting for something in the blistering hot air.

For seven dollars, and after showing our passports, we get an hour's tour. The world's history and the world's fears, lined up, wing to wing: bombers, fighters, patrol planes. Hundreds of every model, in seemingly endless rows. Your brain keeps telling you that this is some game of mirrors, but they're really there. The elderly bus driver exclaims: "Two-thirds of these planes can fly again, and one-third is going to!"

To look at them, you wouldn't say they were especially enthusiastic to get back in the air.

The Boneyard, they call it. A storage site for out-of-service airplanes, while someone decides whether to do something with them or simply dismantle them. There are several such boneyards in Arizona, because climatic conditions in the desert reduce the risk of corrosion. There's one in Phoenix, another in Kingman, and the biggest one is here in Tucson. Parked planes, covered with a coating of mastic tape to protect glass and paint; partially dismantled planes; airplanes on sale, ready to be sent off to poorer countries with lower levels of technology.

Bruce, age seventy-four, drives an open tram through the museum proper: different airplanes, same sunshine beating down. He was an air force pilot, and he lists the names with competence and pride: "DF-8A Crusader! F-105D Thunderchief! F-101B Voodoo! That right there is a C-130, they still make them today! That one was used in the Berlin airlift, to break Stalin's blockade! This one brought the American hostages back from Iran! That one shot down some of the bad guys! Look at the bombs painted on the fuselage, one for every bombing raid!"

The tour is detailed and hot. After an hour and fifteen minutes, the tour group is starting to show signs of exhaustion. Suddenly, mutiny: half of them get up and ask to get out, eager to flee to someplace air-conditioned. My son orders them not to move. He's right. Bruce would have his feelings hurt. He couldn't imagine that anyone could fail to grasp the poetry of row after row of B-52s in the desert.

///////////////////

From Tucson, sun-kissed and geometric, we head north, along geometric, sun-kissed roads. After a long family negotiation, we decide how to choose the soundtrack. Five songs apiece from the iPhone, plugged into the car stereo, I propose. Antonio accepts, and chooses five unsettling rap songs; when it's my turn, he immediately argues with my first choice, and we go back to the radio: someone else can do the choosing for us. As usual, it's country music.

For three days, I suggest, let's be tourists. Antonio is suspicious: he fears an ambush of some kind, a way of trying to get him to learn something. We drive north through Arizona on a state route (77). We stop on the land of the White Mountain Apache tribe (Fort Apache) to admire a Corvette rally, sports cars driven by euphoric seventy-year-olds. We photograph the Painted Desert and we walk out into the Petrified Forest, where my cowboy hat helps me to fit in with the French and German tourists.

The next morning we climb down through the tamarisks and oaks into the Canyon de Chelly, where the ancient Anasazi dug their homes out of the rock cliffs. Red dirt, white rocks, green plants: a damp microclimate, very different from the surrounding desert. Deswood Yazzie, an authorized Navajo guide, shows up in a beat-up Chevrolet Silverado, which he can exit only by pulling the handle on the outside of the door. He leads the way, speaking rarely. I understand; we're seeing what tens of thousands of travelers before us have seen. But I'm seeing it with my son, and that makes all the difference.

I guess that sums up the privilege of being a father. You see everything for the first time, because, at least for a moment, you see things with your children's eyes. Antonio is twenty, my age when I first came to Arizona, with five friends, in a motor home. I was very excited then. But I'm more excited now. Friends travel together for all sorts of reasons—sharing expenses, making the best of time off school. A grown-up son takes to the road with his dad for one reason only: because the two get along and enjoy each other's company. Of course, Antonio would never say it. But we both know it to be true, and that's enough.

Traveling through Many Farms and Rough Rock, that afternoon we reach Navajo National Monument, a place with perfect profiles, where it's impossible to take a bad picture. Monument Valley is not just a place where movies have been made (seven movies by John Ford alone, including *Stagecoach*). Car companies, too, have plundered the imagery of ocher buttes against a blue sky for their ads for the latest model of off-road vehicle. For several billion people around the globe, this is the American West, just as the Colosseum is Italy and the Eiffel Tower is France. In certain matters, mankind is not very sophisticated.

When Ortensia and I lived in Washington, DC, we came out here on vacation. We have a photo of us from that trip, close together and smiling, with the Mitten and Merrick buttes right behind us. What we didn't know was that, just a short while later, Antonio would arrive. Now he's here, driving the Toyota down the track between the rocks and asking Navajo for directions, and this strikes me as wonderful, a circle that folds back on itself. In the immense, recently opened cafeteria-with-a-view, we meet a couple from Piacenza. They tell me that they have a son Antonio's age, who stayed in Italy. "You're very lucky to be traveling with your son," the father tells me. "I know," I reply, when the son in question is out of earshot.

At night, we stop in Flagstaff and have dinner at the Crown Railroad Cafe, where an electric train runs tirelessly around the dining room over the heads of the diners. Route 66 runs through here, and the tourism offerings are all in the nostalgia vein: music and images of an America that no longer exists, intended for foreign tourists and Americans of a certain age. After dinner we go to the Museum Club, which isn't far away. The name worries Antonio: museum? Don't worry, I reassure him. The Web site summarizes for me: "The Museum Club is a historic landmark built in 1931. . . . It was at one time the largest log cabin in Arizona." Every night, it offers live music. Seven dollars at the door, neon lights behind the counter, barstools and pool tables. A heavyset guy about my age is teaching a young woman about Antonio's age how to play. She bends over the table, angling her cue for a difficult shot, and he rubs her back: that's not his daughter. The manager gestures in my direction: "Is the boy twenty-one? No? Then he can't come near the bar, and he has to leave the club by ten p.m." Why? I ask.

"Rules. Arizona State Liquor Board," he replies. So a twenty-year-old in the U.S. can vote, drive, and fight a war, but he can't drink a beer with his father? "That's it," he says, delighted that the foreigner got the point so quickly.

The twenty-year-old can also buy himself a firearm, we discover the following morning. Gary and Coleen Reeder run a gun shop, the Pistol Parlour. Inside I count a bear, a buffalo, and two coyotes, all preserved by the taxidermist's art; also, seven terrier puppies (these are alive). The mass-produced handguns are made by Glock, Ruger, and Colt. The personalized handguns have livelier names: Judge & Jury, Widow-maker, Vampyre Slayer. The Reeders very courteously explain Arizona law to me: after a few quick background checks, at age eighteen a young man can buy a long rifle, and at twenty-one, a handgun or an assault weapon. Interested? No, thanks: my son is normal.

////////////////

We head south toward Phoenix on the I-17. The radio informs us that today is both Cyndi Lauper's and Dan Brown's birthday. Then we head west. For the first time, the GPS navigator is willing to utter the name "San Diego." We get on 85 South: a deserted landing strip, basically, but the speed limit is still sixty-five. Antonio drives, champing at the bit, while I keep an eye on the speedometer.

In Gila Bend, the heat turns surreal. We walk into the only McDonald's as if it were an oasis. We greet the Wi-Fi like a cool breeze. We fill up the tank at a Love's gas station, and then head for Yuma through a range of black mountains. Theba, Sentinel, Aztec, Dateland, Tacna, Ligurta. You get the impression that the way they chose the names of places, in America, is that someone grabbed a dictionary and a globe and jabbed a finger down at random. Then you find out that, in many cases, that's exactly what happened.

As we enter the city, Antonio informs me that Yuma is the sunniest place on earth, according to the Guinness World Records. Out of 4,456 hours of daylight each year, the sun shines there for 4,019 hours. In other words, if you step out onto the street, you know that nine times out of ten, you're at risk of being broiled. Today is well within the statistical median.

There's no change in the landscape as we cross the border into California. America starts to clean up and repopulate only as you approach the Pacific coastline. At the Jaime Obeso Sunbeam Rest Area, the restrooms are impeccable, the drinking water is plentiful, the maps are informative, and the palm trees are luxuriant. The fleeing Mexicans, when they arrive here, no doubt think it's a mirage. At Descanso—San Diego is drawing nearer—we start to see more units of the U.S. Border Patrol, and then we run into a roadblock. Spike strips in the roadway, police dogs in cages, spotlights. At that point, the Mexicans won't have any doubts: they've come to the right place. The ocean and the money are both in that direction.

In San Diego, home of the margarita and the Caesar salad, destination of conformist conference-goers and a haven for sun-caramelized matrons, a hotel room awaits us with a view of the sunset: the direction we've been facing ever since we left. We've crossed America, but we can't stop for long. There's a train to catch, heading north.

The Coast Starlight

On a summer morning in the lobby of a twenty-eight-story hotel next to the ocean, there's no telling what will emerge from the elevators next. Overperfumed young women, noisy children and exhausted mothers, salesmen with their array of samples, Snooki look-alikes, and sculptural Hillary Clinton–style pantsuits. Athletic parents hard at work, in their phosphorescent exercise outfits, and motorcyclists ready to peel out, helmets in hand. Babies crying. Democrats and Republicans, identifiable by their T-shirts: "California for Obama." "Keep Calm and Return Fire!"

Antonio points out a young blonde in flip-flops, wet hair, eyes down-cast, carrying three huge Bloody Marys: a busy night, we have to guess. A woman with a laptop under her arm announces her intention to Skype her hundred-year-old mother who lives in the desert in Arizona and wants to see the ocean. Frank, a builder, tells us that he's a cousin of the boxer Rocky Marciano and asks us to give his regards to Italy.

It's as if America were tilted west and everyone rolled down to San Diego for the weekend. A national assortment of practicality and slop-piness, naïveté and entitlement, bags under eyes and silence, nudity and modesty, excess and repentance. It would be nice to stay here, sitting across from the elevators, and study it. Or else leave the hotel and go back to Mission Bay with a Segway. Antonio, who'd never driven one in his life, took five minutes to learn how, while I, who had experience with the contraption, wound up in a flower bed. Or go back to Petco Park to watch a baseball game, like we did last night: the Padres versus the Phillies. Or perhaps I should say, to watch a ballpark full of Americans eating, drinking, chomping, sucking, rending, gnawing, and swallowing as *they* watch a baseball game. Coca-Cola $9.99! Buy One and Refill All Game! Churro! Jumbo Size! Cracker Jack! Soft Cone! At any given moment, there are dozens of people getting up, sitting back down, walking in all directions. The rhythmic working of jaw and epiglottis marks the passage of time in American sports.

But we can't do any of these things again, nor can we try any new things. Today we have to return our car, and tomorrow morning we have to hit the (rail)road.

//////////////////

Pacific Surfliner: the Americans seem to have a certain gift for naming trains. It departs San Diego at 6:05; we're at Union Station at 5:30 a.m. Antonio is resigned, but not sad. It's a good time of day to play Ruzzle against his friends back in Italy and at this time of the morning, even *Papà* won't try to start a conversation.

Track 10A, on-time departure. We roll along behind the houses, heading north. We discover California as it wakes up, sleepy-eyed in underwear, coffee on the table. Volunteer flowers, palm trees, bougainvilleas, warehouses, parking lots, courtyards, large storage facilities, where Americans, between moves, wait for the recent past to become the distant past. And then there are the trailer parks full of campers, trailers, and motor homes, where the border between traveler and vagrant grows thinner and thinner.

Signs stream by, and I take note of the words. It's a summary of America, with nothing missing. Bruce Springsteen, without needing to add a single verb, could turn it into a song.

Now Leasing	Goodwill Donation
For Rent	Bob Stall Chevrolet
Rio Vista	Pick Up Stick
Bed Bubbles	Babies R Us
Capital Group	99c Only Store
Think Taco Bell!	Smooth FM 98.1
Qualcomm Stadium	Liquor Mart
Café Socrates	American Weddings
The Home Depot	$4.99 Combos!
Cash Back	Food 4 Less
Alvarado Med Center	Boat World
Joel Tires	Atlas Electric Co.

A business litany that turns into a mantra. A predictability that conjures up usage, custom, routine: the new arrivals are immediately captured by the lexicon. A lowest common denominator that is hard to describe—I explain to Antonio, who's baffled by my early-morning flights of philosophy—but it's a challenge that needs to be faced, if we want to understand where it is we've wound up. Nations consist of repetitions more than exceptions.

///////////////

The train personnel remind me, in their speech and manners, of summer camp counselors trying to manage crowds of inept children. The train attendant is called Delores. I ask her how to raise the top bunk. *Step back! Stand by the door! Do it again!* She seems impatient, and I can understand that. In fact, there are travelers who seem to defy logic and patience. The young woman with black hair, for instance, looks worried: she doesn't know how to move her enormous suitcase. I whisper, in Italian: "Why not try pushing it? Or are the wheels strictly decorative?" With Antonio, by this point, all it takes is a glance to communicate. The glance he shoots me says: "Can you mind your own business, even just once?"

We pass Solana Beach, Oceanside, San Juan Capistrano, Irvine, Santa Ana, Anaheim, and Fullerton. In Los Angeles after an hour and twenty minutes spent waiting in an imperially proportioned train station waiting room, practically Soviet in dimensions—we board the Coast Starlight for Seattle, where it is scheduled to arrive tomorrow night at 8:37. A sheet of paper informs us that this is the only train in the entire Amtrak system equipped with a Parlour Car, a panoramic lounge car reserved for sleeping car travelers. "That's us!" I say contentedly.

Between Ventura and Santa Barbara the Coast Starlight, true to its name, hugs the coastline. The marine layer, the early-morning California fog, burns away, to be replaced by blue sky. We meet Reginald and his wife, Gloria. They live in San Diego, and that's where they boarded the train this morning. They're going to Idaho for a conference on electric motors; he's an enthusiastic inventor of same. It'll take them three days to get there.

Gloria wants to chat with us. She loves Marcello Mastroianni and she's curious.

"Have you ever seen a UFO?"

"Maybe I have, but no one told me it was a UFO."

"I have, in my backyard. Did you know they can control our minds?"

"Ah."

"They travel through time. They've been watching us for centuries. A friend of ours was taken aboard by one."

"I see."

"NASA is well aware that Apollo 11 was followed every second of the way by a UFO."

"And how do you know that?"

"They told us so at a convention in Vegas."

The California we see from the train is an unusual one. The train runs along the ocean, past sand and rocks covered with white foamy waves, dirt roads. South of San Luis Obispo, we see farmworkers harvesting vegetables and strawberries, their pickup trucks parked beside the fields. At the station, a short no-smoking stop: you can get out, but you can't smoke a cigarette.

A young Chinese couple is traveling with their child, his face concealed underneath an immense trapper's hat. Elisa is methodically tossing back glasses of zinfandel: she's an artist, she tells us, and she lives in Kansas. Chelsea, on the other hand, comes from a small town near Dallas. This is the first time she's set foot on a train, and she likes it. Devin, who is traveling with her, agrees. He's a mechanic who works on diesel engines. There's a tattoo on his arm: *No Hatred*. He loves Italian poetry, he tells me. I smile, but I don't listen. I am too busy watching as the sun sinks into the ocean, bidding farewell to this last strip of continent.

In my eyes [the berth] is the perfect thing, perfect in conception and execution, this small green hole in the dark moving night, this soft warren in a hard world.

This opinion of E. B. White's strikes me as excessively enthusiastic, especially after I came frighteningly close to crushing my fingers in the foldaway sleeper bunk during the so-called room transformation (from sleeping compartment to sitting compartment, and back again). The process is illustrated in the pamphlet issued to every passenger (*Coast Starlight® Welcome Aboard*). The Americans aren't shy about showing how things work. If anything, they find such illustrations to be admirable, verging on the poetic: they are a demonstration of how the world operates.

In any case, it's true. There's something old-fashioned and reassuring about falling asleep while in movement. It's fascinating to look out the window while lying down. A train is neither a plane nor a ship: what's going past out there is other people's lives, not just clouds and waves.

It's the last night of our trip. Antonio is fast asleep in the bottom bunk. I watch America go past in the darkness as we pull out of Oakland, where we stopped to say hello to some friends. The train heads east until Sacramento; then it turns north. Chico, Redding, the Oregon state line. First stop in Oregon: Klamath Falls, scheduled arrival at 8:17 a.m.

//////////////////////

How nice to wake up in the forest, with the blue sky peeking down from between the green trees, with the mountains in the distance. Every so often a lake zips past, between the trees. Beauty in motion, but glimpsing it from cubicle 12 in car 1431 is no easy matter, during the day.

The upper bunk, in fact, is a gurney smashed up against the ceiling: it's impossible to sit up. To get your clothing, you have to slither like a contortionist and extract it from the netting screwed to the wall. Trains, I find myself thinking, are useful: they prepare you for life and beyond. Anyone who has tried Amtrak is ready to deal with prison, a field hospital, or a submarine, or perhaps even being buried. I lean over to say good morning to Antonio: "If you want to know what fatherly love means, just consider the fact that I gave you the lower bunk." He replies with a grunt. Good: he knows it.

When we get up—my son is never in a hurry, in these cases—I note a frantic whir of activity. Invitations to make reservations for breakfast and a great quantity of other information explode out of the loudspeakers positioned just inches from our ears. There's a sort of sadistic euphoria in the voices of announcers aboard trains and ships. It must be simply electrifying, the knowledge that you're addressing a large number of people who are forced to listen. Come to think of it, that must be the feeling experienced by managing directors at corporate retreats and heads of household at Thanksgiving dinners.

A train isn't a vehicle: it's a place. A place where people don't like to shut up. Talkativeness, I think as the Coast Starlight cuts across the Winema National Forest, is inversely proportional to velocity. On the Frecciarossa express from Rome to Milan, everyone's busy and silent; on the Amtrak Coast Starlight, massive and slow, they're quiet only when they're asleep. In the Parlour Car—the name a foreshadowing—the same thing happens: we find ourselves talking with perfect strangers. In America—I catch myself thinking—railway conversation is also a way of saving money. People use their traveling companions as free psychoanalysts. They sit there listening, every once in a while they have something to say, and if you want, you never have to see them again.

///////////////

The Wi-Fi appears, like an oasis in the telecommunications desert, and then vanishes just as suddenly. Two travelers are talking about sports, two others are talking about Obama, and a little girl is playing with her blond hair. Behind us monumental pine forests go streaming past. A married couple talks about whether it's appropriate to use a cane on the train; then they move on to a discussion of the pointlessness of having restaurant staff learn languages. ("They're all Mexicans or Italians, and they know a little English. What more do they need?") A French teacher, who studied at Berkeley, breaks into the conversation. A man in his early thirties with a red beard that you'd expect to see on a prophet pulls out a deck of cards and asks the young woman sitting across from him if she'd care for a game. I realize that, hidden behind her hand of cards, there is a tiny baby in a Snugli, completely uninterested in the game of poker.

I look for my own baby boy. Two seats down, there he is, playing Plants vs. Zombies. I walk over, waving a copy of the Klamath Falls *Herald and News*. An extraterrestrial landing in America who wants to know how people live, I say, ought to just buy a local daily. Not for the news—it's the same everywhere—but for the ads. Since it's summer, there's a lot of attention to lawn mowers, hedge trimmers, coolers, and grills (starting at $149.99). There's even a tiny swimming pool ($289.99) someone managed to cram ten people into. The names of the products being touted are invariably epic. A can of exterior paint ($21.99) is called Dirt Fighter. The cheapest sleeping bag ($14.99) is Glacier's Edge. A girl's bike ($99.99) is the Carolina Cruiser; the boy's equivalent, at the same price, is a Cliff Runner (exactly the place where a boy in Oregon should NOT be riding his bike).

Antonio looks at me: *Can't you just read a newspaper like everyone else? Or maybe* not *read one, like me?*

//////////////////

We arrive in Eugene, Oregon, around noon. Vickie, the Amtrak attendant, announces: anyone who gets out does so at their own risk. "People get out for a cigarette," she explains, "they lose track of time, and then they have to spend a hundred ten dollars for a taxi, the only way to catch up with the Coast Starlight in Portland."

"I'm a vegetarian, but with one exception: bacon!" my neighbor one seat over suddenly exclaims. I don't point out that she's changed the subject; I just ask if she likes hers crunchy.

We arrive in Portland, Oregon. All we see of the rainiest, greenest (most environmental) city in America, full of roses and charmingly intolerant people, is the train station. At six in the evening, we're in

Olympia, at seven we're in Tacoma, and at eight thirty we pull into Seattle, King Street Station. We get off the train and say farewell to the Coast Starlight, which continues on to Vancouver, British Columbia. We sit outside the station with our suitcases, looking over at the Seattle Seahawks' stadium, waiting for our friends Diego and Monica.

We did it: we were in Washington, DC, and now we're in Washington State. We traveled from the Atlantic to the Pacific, by way of the Gulf of Mexico. We went through fifteen states, eleven major cities, and traveled 5,003.5 miles: 2,513 miles by train, 525 by bus, 1,923 by car, 19 by subway, another 19 by boat, and 4.5 on a Segway.

We've arrived. My son has carried me here. Without him, I would never have embarked on a journey like this.

Antonio smiles: he knows it.

2

From Berlin to Palermo: A Vertical Europe

The old houses streaked past us, we could see
lighted windows in the dark courtyards and in the rooms—
it was a matter of seconds—there seemed to be men
and women bending over parcels, closing suitcases.
Or was it all my imagination?

DINO BUZZATI, "CATASTROPHE"

Dueling Suitcases

I meet Mark Spörrle. He's the journalist—from Hamburg, as it turns out—whom the Goethe-Institut, Germany's worldwide cultural institute, paired with me. Their idea is to have an Italian and a German travel together, and see what comes of it. He's taller than me, stronger than me, and younger than me, and has a suitcase that weighs twice as much as mine. If our journey is meant to demolish the stereotypes of Germans and Italians, then we're starting badly.

On the other hand, if we're talking about attitude, there we're doing well. Mark seems happy to board a train in Berlin and get out in Palermo, just as I am. Certainly, it might be a sign of wobbly mental health. But writers are strange people, whatever the latitude.

In the hotel, before our departure, we challenge each other in front of the video camera: who can empty his suitcase and describe its contents in ninety seconds? The operation unfolds before the eyes of the customers in the bar of the art'otel berlin mitte (that's how it's written, lowercase letters and all). The baffled eyes, I should add: they've never seen an Italian and a German count undershirts and boxer shorts in a public establishment before, certainly not at aperitif time. By the way, for an eight-day trip, he has brought eight shirts, eight undershirts, eight pairs of underpants. My numbers are more . . . artistic.

In the time available to us before we catch our German train heading south, Mark convinced me to board one means of public transportation after another, transferring all over Berlin like a busking violinist in search of spare change: U-Bahn, S-Bahn, and trolleys all the way out to Marzahn, the eastern outskirts where Communist apartment buildings have been painted, the streets spruced up, and young women are capable of freezing passersby with a glance (they must have learned it from mothers and grandmothers, who were well trained in the years of the German Democratic Republic). An instructive setting, where we could bring schoolchildren on field trips from all over Europe. Here we have proof that Communism is an absurd idea: if even the Germans couldn't make it work, it simply can't work.

These days, the neighborhood is inhabited by Asian immigrants, indigenous Fascist skinheads, aging Communists who have requested that a monument be erected to Erich Honecker. (A paltry herd of metal deer, because the East German leader had his hunting reserve around here. If it makes them happy . . .) I visited a youth center here called Betonia—roughly translated, Concretia—in honor of cement. I even went up to see the Pension 11 Himmel (eleventh heaven; Germans think a seventh heaven isn't enough), in an apartment building of perfect German Socialist style. A curious place: the interior decoration seems to have been done by Little Red Riding Hood after a brawl with Michael Jackson. It costs eleven euros a night, breakfast included.

In the afternoon, Mark, determined to educate me about Germany, takes me to Spandau, stronghold of the capital's middle class. We go to visit a Futternapf outlet, the leading chain of pet stores; it seems that this Futternapf store has a higher sales volume (including products sold on the installment plan) than any other retail outlet in Germany, and doesn't know the meaning of downturn. I meet parrots with a Wagnerian gaze; I visit gymnasiums for cats; I examine food meant for pythons. This will be helpful preparation for our Italian journey, I tell Mark. Maybe Goethe did the same thing, but he never wrote about it.

At noon, a pause for lunch on the seventh floor of the Kaufhaus des Westens—familiarly known as the KaDeWe—a major department store that makes an Italian La Rinascente look like a roadside grill and Harrods, a Middle Eastern bazaar. This is the amusement park frequented by well-to-do elderly Berliners with time on their hands. They move like jerky footage from a hand-cranked movie camera and order ponderously from waitresses who serve them in slow motion. They have traces of youth in their eyes or their hair; but they'd already started a family when, on the other side, the East Germans built the Wall. But so far, nobody's knocked them down.

My New Car! I'm About to Cry

A hundred trains a day! Fourteen tracks on four levels! The Berlin Hauptbahnhof is so intensely functional that it can stir any traveler's soul. Except for a German traveler. Mark is widely known as a sarcastic critic of his country's railways (Deutsche Bahn, or DB). Today he lives up to his reputation: he assures me that many Berliners preferred the old railway station, and he insists that first-class sections of trains are occasionally left out beyond the platform cantilever awnings, forcing the travelers to get drenched in the rain.

Maybe so, but it strikes me as a magnificent place. I'm almost sorry to leave—in part because the minute we do depart, we're surrounded by kids: high school students from Stuttgart, on their way back from a field trip to the capital. They come in making noise, trade seats, shout names and requests. But they must have been out all night, because they fall asleep almost instantly. Thirty sixteen-year-olds with their eyes closed, as if under a spell. Since I have work to do, I silently thank the Good Fairy.

Our train departs; besides Mark and yours truly, there is Soledad Ugolinelli, who is in charge of translation and logistics, and Gianni Scimone, who is responsible for keeping a video diary of the trip. The train runs from Berlin to Basel, but today we're going to get out at Wolfsburg, where Mark—if I've understood correctly—has organized a courteous and complicated reception. We arrive on time (of course); we are told that a fifth of the state of Saxony works for Volkswagen or for allied industries (naturally); everything appears spotless and efficient (predictably). Even the lost-luggage office is operational, though that's the realm where uncertainty reigns in train stations around the world. The only contrivance that's out of order is the conveyor belt running along next to the stairways. Apparently someone put his child on the belt instead of a suitcase, and that jammed up the works.

AUTOSTADT, the city of cars, proclaims a sign by the river. The leading tourist attraction in all of Lower Saxony. Volkswagen: cars for the people! Every day some three thousand Volkswagen vehicles are manufactured here. Six hundred a day are handed over to customers who come here from all over Germany to pick them up. They save on shipping costs to the dealership, but they spend just as much to enjoy the experience. And so, I ask myself, why do they do it?

But then I actually witness the ritual of the delivery, and I understand: a German industrial symphony, for which I, too, would be willing to pay the price of admission. A screen lights up, announcing the customer's name, the model of vehicle, and the exact time of delivery, which takes place in an atmosphere of intense emotion. The new owners take pictures, record videos, pose next to their shiny new purchase. Families with children approach the new car as if it were a miraculous apparition. It may be the perfection of the various mechanisms, the little lakes, or perhaps the flowers, but I almost expect a thunderous voice from on high to announce: "I am Volkswagen, your carmaker! You shall have no other carmakers before me!"

But that doesn't happen. Only peaceful sunbeams shaft in through the glass, lovingly illuminating the Polos and Passats ready to begin their new lives.

How to Miss a German Train and Live Happily Ever After

After an excursion to Hötensleben, population 2,650, a perfectly preserved memorial to the border with the GDR, a person feels better. Is this marketing of bad memories? No: it's a warning to future generations. Not only did we see a chunk of the Wall (with a capital *W*), but we also managed to avoid slamming into a wall (lowercase). The driver, a German of Romanian descent with a vague resemblance to Michael Caine after a hard night out on the town, displayed a distinct animosity toward traffic lights, and tended to ignore them. When we pointed this out to him, he replied: "I've taken a safe-driving course." A safe-driving course! We offer him our heartfelt congratulations. Never contradict whoever's at the wheel, especially along the steep and winding roads of Saxony-Anhalt.

Train no. 873 departs Wolfsburg at 3:40 p.m. for Göttingen, where eleven Nobel laureates studied. Then a regional train for Weimar, where Goethe and Schiller lived, and, sometime later, a failing republic made way for a rising housepainter. The train is packed. I arrive in the carriage out of breath—second class; Mark considers first class to be a sign of morbid weakness—and look around for a place to plug in my computer. I find it immediately and mentally extend my congratulations to the Germans for their railway efficiency. But I discover that the outlet is dead. There's no electricity. A stranger approaches me. He introduces himself, gives me his business card. He's an engineer who's built railroads in Egypt, Qatar, South America, and Siberia. He suggests sticking a pencil into the outlet, "to reset the fuse." A pencil? I ask. A pencil, he confirms. I do as I'm told. It works! What a country Germany is. They put technicians in second class to help passengers.

I have only one criticism of Teutonic efficiency. Mark really ought to take a look every now and then at the timetable and, while he's at it, at his watch. At 1:09 p.m., the scheduled time of departure from Weimar printed on the ticket, after our visit to the Goethehaus (Goethe's House), we're in a restaurant struggling to down a gigantic sausage, a Thüringer Rostbratwurst. As a result, we miss our train for Fulda, the connecting train for Munich, and all our reservations. I suspect that Herr Spörrle did it on purpose just to convince me that the Germans aren't all that precise after all. But I'm not falling for it: I'm convinced they went so far as to organize a state of disorganization, as a gesture of hospitality. They just wanted to make me feel at home.

⁄⁄⁄⁄⁄⁄⁄⁄⁄⁄⁄⁄⁄⁄

At last, we reach Munich. We take rooms at the Fleming's Hotel in Schwabing, where I can devote myself to the study of the German spirit (hotel division).

FIRST POSTULATE

Four-star hotels in Germany can be split into two categories: efficient and extremely efficient. Everything will work—Internet, shower, thermostat, television, erotic movies added to your bill under the heading "Media Package"—but you're going to have to figure out how to work them on your own. No one will help you. The young women at the front desk won't offer explanations. Their idea of service entails three steps: (a) Fill out the form! (b) Take the key! (c) Now beat it because I'm busy!

SECOND POSTULATE

On your bed in an Italian hotel room, you will find one pillow and one blanket. On German beds you'll find a series of objects, some of them soft, where you can lay your head; and two narrow goose-down quilts, which meet in the center of the bed and are designed to slide sideways over the course of the night. Don't complain! Instead, simply try to collect all the covers you can find (on the bed, in the closets and wardrobes), pile them up, and climb under, adopting the method of the Indians of the Great Lakes region.

THIRD POSTULATE

Many Germans don't know how to peel a Weisswurst, but you must pretend to be more inept than they are. Beating them at the task would be a needless humiliation: it's as if a friend from Hamburg came to Italy and understood before you did how to twirl spaghetti on a fork. Important point: during breakfast (*das Frühstück*) load your plate as if you had just finished a hunger strike (eggs, sausages, cheeses, smoked fish, cold cuts, cucumbers, and a bunch of other indigestible items). Emit grunts of satisfaction. Then, when no one can see you, leave everything on the table and hurry off to order an espresso.

How to Deal with Railway Germany

This morning, after breakfast, a short tour of the capital of Bavaria. The city, which I first visited in long-ago 1978, and which I've seen many times since, is pleasantly Southern. Behind Marienplatz there are forests of asparagus for sale and lots of visiting tourists. The Nordic Herr Spörrle was born in Flensburg, practically in Denmark, and he observes the confusion in the streets with some amusement. I ask for a Weisswurst, which was invented here in 1857 as a way of recycling waste meat. It's almost one o'clock in the afternoon, so I really shouldn't: these delicate white sausages—Mark explains, as I begin to discover his didactic side—should be eaten only before noon. This was required by an age-old law, for hygienic considerations bound up with the raw materials, and the law stated that violators would have their fingers chopped off. I look around, but all the Bavarians I see have unchopped hands.

At 1:31 p.m. another train awaits us. We will leave this interesting (German) south and descend to the (Italian) north, by way of Austria. At the main Munich station (Hauptbahnhof), the police have shut off access to the tracks ahead of us: a bomb threat, apparently. Mark remains unflappable. I see greater signs of alarm, however, when his father, Günter, appears unannounced. Günter Spörrle is an actor by profession and lives here in Munich. He has a regular role in *Tatort* (Crime Scene), the longest-running German television drama. In this situation, Spörrle Senior is behaving like a good papa: he brings us muesli bars and plenty of water.

While the Spörrle family carries out its traditional rituals, and we prepare to say farewell to the Germanic universe, here are a few pieces of advice for anyone who might choose to emulate our experience.

Germany by Train

INSTRUCTIONS FOR SELF-DEFENSE

1. ALLOW PLENTY OF TIME TO BUY YOUR TICKETS from the automatic vending machines. They operate like Kant's *Critique of Pure Reason*; but if high school philosophy is a distant memory, they're quite capable of throwing you off. The procedure is time-consuming, and if there is a pack of travelers in a hurry muttering behind you, it can become unnerving. One good way of settling the matter is to lean your forehead against the metal and burst into tears: someone will come to your aid. Well, if you're a dark-haired young woman from Florence, this ploy will certainly work. For a silver-haired Lombard in his fifties, on the other hand, it might not.

2. TURN OFF THE RINGER ON YOUR CELL PHONE. If someone calls you and you're on a train, don't answer. Avoid conversations
any longer than ten seconds. If it's something urgent, rather than facing
a wall of silent collective disapproval, lock yourself in one of the restrooms (the restrooms on the ICE, or Intercity-Express, trains are full
of Italians, Frenchmen, and Spaniards talking animatedly about love
and business). On German trains the normal Latin practice—sharing
your personal business with the rest of the car, who in return offer comments and advice—is vigorously discouraged.

3. IF YOU HAVE A COMPUTER, USE IT (check your mail, watch
a movie). If you have a book or a newspaper, read it. If you have cookies, eat them. If you have a fruit juice, drink it. If you brought a Battle-
ship board game, play it (without making whooshing noises for the
launching of the torpedoes). If you're sleepy, get some sleep (or at least
yawn). The important thing is to *do* something. Inactivity, especially if
combined with watchful observance of one's neighbor, is viewed with
suspicion.

4. MAKE AN EFFORT TO SPEAK A LITTLE GERMAN. It is a
sweet and logical language, but you pretend you find it harsh and difficult. Nothing can stir the soul of a German teacher—they're everywhere; don't dream of being able to avoid them—like a foreigner who
doesn't know how to pronounce "*wahrscheinlich.*"

5. DON'T TRY TO BE FUNNY. The railway staff in Germany wear
magnificent red caps. It is forbidden to take one home as a souvenir. If
you absolutely cannot resist, offer to barter some item of headgear
brought with you from Venice. I almost forgot: warn the other party
before substituting one item of headgear for the other. Deutsche Bahn
AG might not look kindly upon one of their conductors wearing a straw
gondolier hat.

The Mystical German and a Cheese-Driven Ecstasy

At the Brenner Pass I purchase a copy of *La Gazzetta dello Sport*, to prepare for my reentry into Italy. Here the young people are already shouting at a volume that is imperceptibly higher than that of Munich, and decidedly louder than in Berlin. At last, we reach Bolzano, our first stop in Italy. Mark darts out of the train, emerges into the alpine sunlight, sniffs at the wind, and shouts ecstatically: *"Die Luft! Die Luft!* The air, the air!"

There we go, I think silently: *We've lost another one.*

And that's just the beginning. You should see him in the afternoon, at the facilities of the Panini family in Modena, leaning into the transcendent depths of cheese making. His gaze is filled with a wild surmise at the ranked choirs and dominions of aged Parmesan cheese. A majestic spectacle, an intoxicating scent. Friedrich Hölderlin would have sat down and composed a poem on the spot, but Mark Spörrle just heaves an ecstatic sigh.

I've chosen Modena as our second stop, because it's a concentrate of the chewiest Italy (prosciutto, gnocco fritto), the most precise Italy (engines, automobiles), and the fizziest Italy (Lambrusco, personality). Mark puts up no resistance: he seems to be won over; he doesn't try to convince me that Wolfsburg is better.

Struck amidships and sent straight to the bottom, Herr Spörrle! In Germany you explained the virtues of German organization. Now allow me to illustrate the characteristics of the Italian genius.

1. *Example.* From art, business, and fashion to precision mechanics, literature, and fine foods: good examples bring good results. Imitation and emulation are forms of instruction. In Italy, we live in a double boiler of beauty and imagination. Our historic cities, our clothing, our dining. The surrounding environment is a stimulus and a challenge: we are forced to gauge the things we do against what preceded us.

2. *Effort.* "In Italy, for thirty years under the Borgias, they had warfare, terror, murder, and bloodshed, but they produced Michelangelo, Leonardo da Vinci, and the Renaissance. In Switzerland, they had brotherly love, they had five hundred years of democracy and peace—and what did that produce? The cuckoo clock." In the peevishness of the statement (from the great film *The Third Man*, by the way), there's still a grain of truth, and it has to do with us: challenges have never hindered our creativity. The results of Italian scientific research—done with limited funds and lots of red tape—prove it. Our university graduates do well outside the country in part because they had to measure up against Italian universities. Anyone who emerges from the labyrinth and finds the open highway will travel straight and far.

3. *Mixing.* The Italians view uncontrolled immigration with understandable apprehension. But this they know: due to factors of history, geography, and national character, we have succeeded in obtaining advantages from our exchanges and encounters. From the discovery of America to that of the moka pot, from helicopters to typewriters, and from Ferrari (automobiles) to Ferrari (spumantes), Italian creations have never been isolated undertakings, but invariably the result of splendid hybrids.

The Railway Is a Metaphor

Caelum non animum mutant qui trans mare currunt. "They change their sky but not their soul who cross the ocean," wrote Quintus Horatius Flaccus, whom we know as Horace, two thousand years ago. All right, he was talking about ships, not trains. But you get the message. The Italy that travels is no different from the Italy that stays in one place.

From Bolzano to Trento, I talk to the young man working the bar trolley, who loves Americans because they cleaned out his entire stock of alcoholic beverages ("I had to ask for a resupply!"). And he appreciates

Austrians and Germans, who at least do their darnedest. The Italians, on the other hand, don't drink much and when they do, they ask for a discount.

Between Trento and Verona, I meet a retired general from the Alpini division. Having run through his complaints about the state of the nation, he mutters: "Never seen this train so clean in my life. Maybe they know that there are two journalists and a video camera. Come back more often, men."

The whole way from Verona to Modena, while Gianni films the tracks hurtling into the distance behind the train, I talk with Eleonora, a young disabled woman. She tells me that she was accompanied to the carriage, but that, disappointingly, there was no working wheelchair lift. Before becoming disabled, Eleonora drove to Beijing in a Citroën Méhari with a man she met on this very rail line. "We talked for three hours; then he said: 'Do you want to drive to Beijing with me?'"

It was harder than that to persuade Mark that, in order to travel from Modena to Naples, you need to go by way of Milan. To be exact, by way of San Siro stadium, where my team is playing a crucial match tonight. But in the end, I succeeded. Now I'm going to have to explain to him just what soccer is in Italy. I've been trying for the past three days. I prepared a quiz of basic minimum soccer competence, without which entry into a stadium becomes blasphemy. If he fails to pass it, I'll just leave him at the baggage deposit.

An Emergency, *Bitte*

You've got to love him. This man just doesn't know what to come up with anymore to enliven the trip. We get out of the cab in front of the main station of Milan (Stazione Centrale)—it's just a few minutes until the train leaves for Naples—and Mark announces, beatifically, that he's left his iPhone in the taxi. Italian Personal Solidarity (IPS) goes into action, the only form of emergency management that has never to date generated scandals of any kind.

We call the number of the lost phone, hoping someone will pick up. Then the number of the taxi dispatch office, where they track down the young female taxi driver who deposited us at the station. She picks up on the third ring, understands the situation, and generously volunteers to turn around and bring the phone straight back to the Stazione Centrale, so that we can catch our train. The young woman shows up, out of breath, brandishing the object of Teutonic desire. Herr Spörrle is deeply moved. He has recovered his iPhone and we won't have to miss another train. *"L'Italia è meravigliosa!"* he exclaims in Italian. "Italy is wonderful." I think to myself: *True.* Give us an emergency and we're phenomenal. It's routine administration that we seem to have a few problems with.

As does the Stazione Centrale these days, for that matter. No waiting rooms, just a bar, no Wi-Fi, token-operated bathrooms, automatic ticket machines out of order, escalators designed with shops in search of customers in mind, not travelers in a hurry. And it's a pity, because Italy's high-speed trains, the Alta Velocità, are something to be proud of. There's an Italy, bigger and bigger with each passing day, that travels and works at 155 miles per hour. An Italy that's well aware that improvisation is a fine thing, but that efficiency, too, has its advantages.

We pass through Rome's Termini station. We pass through Naples: an alluring female conductor appears who triggers Mark's enthusiasm. He believes that she's a fashion model traveling incognito. In the evening, we arrive in the city of Lamezia Terme, where I immediately realize something: Calabria is going to surprise me more than Germany did, perhaps because I'm less familiar with it. This really takes the cake: I'm going to have to thank the Germans for having convinced me to explore my own country.

Lamezia is not a pretty sight. No one would dream of spending his or her holidays here. Buildings are bare; streets are full of honking cars; neon signs fail to give the place any warmth. But people are friendly. This evening a busload of children from Crotone will arrive in Lamezia to show us that they know tongue twisters in German; the event will be held in a club known as the Flying Baron. I wonder who could have dreamed up such a thing. The long trip and my general weariness have a slight hallucinogenic effect. I have the impression I heard Mark get to his feet in the restaurant and declaim the Italian tongue twister *Apelle figlio d'Apollo*. I ask the woman sitting beside me: it's all true.

Everything Slows Down

At 7:30 a.m. we are displaying great discipline, waiting at the appointed hour with our baggage outside the Aer Hotel Phelipe in Lamezia, which proved to be very welcoming. Mark, no surprise, isn't there. If you ask me, he does it on purpose. He's been ready for half an hour, and he's just hiding somewhere, anxious to prove that German punctuality is a mere stereotype. Which is all well and good, but it's threatening to make us miss the 8:10 a.m. local train to Villa San Giovanni, the tip of the toe of the Italian boot.

Our descent along Calabria's Tyrrhenian (western) coast is slow and ceremonious. The railways around here aren't used to going from one place to another. They're evidence of a state presence and relics of industrial archaeology, which a few inhabitants, who have no alternative, insist on continuing to use. It seems almost vulgar to have a destination, obligations, and a timetable to stick to. Those are things you can do in Germany, if you're so minded.

Mark generously makes it clear: here there are aesthetic, literary, and human consolations, to complement the stunning landscape. It's true. And in fact we meet another beautiful and amiable female conductor, the fourth one in two days. At this point I begin to suspect that Trenitalia—knowing about the video camera—has decided to put out a casting call among its onboard female personnel. Luisa, smiling in her uniform, explains to us that we're wrong: this is her usual route; this is her usual shift; no one assigned her to this run.

We see her again that afternoon—in civilian dress—on the regional train from Messina to Palermo, reading *The Odyssey*. A Calabrian railway employee who looks like Nicole Kidman and loves Homer? It was worth the trip from Berlin, but it strikes us as statistically unlikely. She smiles again: "I'm going to Palermo to visit friends, and I chose this train on purpose. It usually runs late, but today you're on board: two journalists and a video camera. I knew that it would be on time."

Getting there, aboard the Messina–Palermo regional train, wasn't easy. At Villa San Giovanni a sign pointing to Sicily would have been considered far too obvious. The traveler is obliged to wander like a soul in limbo, in search of the ferry. The only indication is a small sign with the words "To the gangway—1st, 2nd, 3rd docking areas" (the word "gangway," *passerella* in Italian, has to be guessed at because someone has erased the second *e* and the double *l*). "After all, everyone already knows," they told us brusquely at the ticket window. The people from Reggio Calabria and Messina, maybe. But the people from Milan and Hamburg don't.

We depart at 10:35 a.m., but our ferry isn't the 10:35 ferry: it's the 9:30 ferry running late. Explaining this concept to Mark takes up the entire length of the crossing, on a Sicilian Strait swept by sun and wind. When we land, the German is in a lyrical mood and has already forgotten everything. We arrive at the Messina Marittima ferry station and push our luggage all the way to Messina Centrale train station, after discovering that there is no convenient transportation from ferry to train. Many trains go zipping by, destination Palermo, but they don't stop: these are Intercity trains from Milan, Rome, and Naples. We come from Calabria: what else do we expect?

The tiny regional train between Messina and Palermo seems like a toy train: little, green, bright, and slow. In its way, spectacular.

Signora Cardani—visibly pregnant, holding a toddler daughter by the hand—is issued a summons for 216 euros for boarding the train without a ticket. It hardly matters that, before our eyes, she informs the conductor that at the station of Patti the ticket office was closed, and the automatic ticket machines were out of order.

In the bathroom we find soft toilet paper emblazoned with butterflies. This, I explain to Mark, who fails to understand my astonishment, is scientifically impossible: in the history of train-riding humanity, no one has ever glimpsed soft toilet paper emblazoned with butterflies aboard a Sicilian regional train. "It's the final, indisputable proof that Trenitalia knows we're aboard this train, and is secretly staging the sets!" I claim in a loud voice in front of the closed door.

"So much the better," replies a young man as he leaves the bathroom.

We pull into Palermo Centrale, right on time. Built in 1885 in an eclectic monumental style, it's one of the oldest continuously operating Italian train stations. To shoot the last moments of our railroad adventure, as soon as we get out of the train, we try to cross Piazza Giulio Cesare. It proves to be the riskiest enterprise of the entire trip: buses parked on the zebra stripes, cars forming barricades, wailing motor scooters that appear out of nowhere and head straight for our ankles.

I watch Mark Spörrle. He's trying to make up his German mind: do I hate this place or do I like it? Thirty seconds. He turns around and smiles. He likes it. Good: let's go have dinner. Food in Palermo is much better than in Berlin, my friend.

3

From Moscow to Lisbon:
A Horizontal Europe

The names of the stations begin to take on meaning
and my heart trembles. The train stamps and stamps onward.
I stand at the window and hold on to the frame.
These names mark the boundaries of my youth.

ERICH MARIA REMARQUE,
ALL QUIET ON THE WESTERN FRONT

In Moscow

I remember Moscow in the summer of 1986. Then I was anxiously boarding a train heading east: after traveling for 5,593 miles, without changing trains, I'd arrive in Beijing, China. This time I'm taking a train heading west. But the Trans-Siberian Express exists; the Trans-European doesn't yet. That doesn't matter, we'll build it ourselves. After 3,930 miles and changing trains several times, I'll reach Lisbon, Portugal.

Back then I was on my honeymoon with Ortensia, my beaming newlywed wife. She hadn't even lost her composure when we learned, at the Moscow Yaroslavskaya station, that we would be traveling and sleeping in a four-bunk compartment for the next eight days. Our two traveling companions were young Russian women accidentally assigned to our second-class sleeping compartment.

This time, too, we would be traveling in a group of four, but intentionally. Departing with me are Mark Spörrle (fellow writer from Germany), Soledad Ugolinelli (our producer from Rome), and Gianni

Scimone (videographer from Milan). The division of responsibilities is simple: Mark and I create problems; Soledad and Gianni solve them.

This morning in Moscow, for instance, here's what we talked about.

A European journey has to be understandable to Europeans. My Italian and Mark's German aren't enough. The Goethe-Institut, which sponsors our trip, took care of our blog, organizing daily translations into the languages of the countries through which we're traveling: Russia, Ukraine, Poland, Czech Republic, Austria, Switzerland, France, Spain, and Portugal. Plus English, which everyone claims to understand. But the videos? Not a simple matter. Do we go with silent movies? Subtitles? Dubbing?

When presented with this last suggestion, our videographer, Gianni, turns pale. Daily translating and dubbing? I, ever the optimist, minimize: "Let's just get started and see what happens!" Mark, ever the pessimist, analyzes, and requests a pause for reflection.

I like German pauses for reflection: they're useful to Italians, who can now go get an espresso and come up with something. Last night Gianni and I shot the introduction to the journey, on Red Square, where preparations are under way for the May Day parade and for the anniversary of the Soviet victory in the Second World War (May 9). I've lived in Moscow; I know that square, but every time I see it, it leaves me speechless: because of the interplay of the slopes, Saint Basil's Cathedral always seems to pop up out of nowhere. Mark had argued against the filming: "They'll never give you permission!" No problem, guy: we just won't ask.

Leaving Moscow

The hotels in this city have three interesting characteristics. Two of those characteristics have remained unchanged since Soviet times: the presence of young ladies of beautiful appearance and less lovely reputation, and staff that is convinced that to smile would be rude. The third characteristic is relatively new and coincides with the rule of Vladimir Putin: Western music, played at full volume, echoing off the marble and the velvet, only to disappear again as quickly as it came. These are dress rehearsals for private parties: pop-rock is a sign of modernity, and the volume is proportional to the wealth.

Another passion that seems to hold the Putinian Russian bourgeoisie firmly in its grip is the love of toying with memories of the USSR. It's not a political nostalgia; it's imperial and generational: deep down, these are childhood memories, from a time when they felt powerful. While the government might make patriotic use of it, others have discovered commercial applications. At the restaurant Mari Vanna, I sit spellbound at the sight of a screen that broadcasts exclusively Soviet television from the sixties and seventies; the waitresses wear long blond braids, and the interior decoration glorifies the achievements of Russian Communism. Even the bouncer is vintage: a guy in a tracksuit at the front door, listening to an old transistor radio.

Russia, which we are preparing to leave today, knows how to be grouchy. But it still remains a nation capable of passion and profundity. It's a Slavic Italy, rough and Nordic: people spend their time looking for shortcuts and work-arounds, and it is parsimonious with the truth, but it's capable of generosity, and resignation. The Russians, even more than us, can put up with anything. The stoicism of this frozen, alcoholic land is unrivaled in Europe.

Because Moscow is Europe. It's a far edge of Europe—in terms of geography, history, and personality—but it's still a Europe we should neither lose nor abandon. A Europe that's been through a long, obtuse Communist dictatorship, and which slid immediately afterward into the most slovenly experiment with democracy of the twentieth century, under the leadership of Boris Yeltsin, only to wind up finally in the skillful and rapacious hands of Vladimir Putin. A Europe tossed between new rules and ancient instincts that has been arguing, for centuries, about what it wants to become. In the Russia of Czar Nicholas I

(1825–1855), the Slavophiles sang the praises of the values of an agrarian, patriarchal nation. The Westernizers (*Zapadniki*) wanted to continue along the reform path first taken by Peter the Great. Read Dostoevsky's *The Idiot*: not much has changed.

The first time I came to Moscow was in 1986; I lived there in 1991; I've come back a dozen or so times since then. I realize that I've become a public menace: there's a danger I might bore everyone with my reminiscences. But I love to see places again, mixing familiarity and surprise. Today, I climb up the Vorobyovy Gory (Sparrow Hills) and find Sunday crowds and snow in May. At the belvedere on the top of the hill, overlooking the Moskva River, vendors are charging 150 euros (not dollars, like in the old days) for a small bust of Leonid Brezhnev that looks very much as if it was manufactured in China a month ago. I object: "Are you serious?" The vendors reply dismissively: "Don't worry about it. It's not meant for you foreigners. This is meant for us Russians, because we have the money."

Arriving in Kiev

The four of us resemble bicycles: to stay upright, we have to keep moving. Two days in Moscow were enough to make it clear that we weren't cut out for tourism. As soon as taxi no. 255 heads off toward the Kiyevskaya station, we catch a whiff of the change of mood. The trans-European journey has begun! Even the city seems a little less hostile, as the neon lights blink on to ward off the sunset.

I have to admit, I like Russian stations. They're full of kiosks that sell old-fashioned products; places to sit; policemen with oversized cinematic hats. You go to the track at the last second, just minutes before departure. When it's cold out, for heat-related reasons. When it's warm out, as it is this evening, just because that's how everyone is used to doing it.

It's still deeply stirring, after years of traveling, to see the word Киев on the departure board. Kiev, Ukraine! Our first stop on the long trip to Lisbon. We board the train. It pulls out into the Moscow night. The woman in charge of the carriage is a statuesque Ukrainian, capable of stopping a speeding locomotive with a glance. She checks to make sure that all is in order, and then moves on.

At four in the morning, we reach the border. Four expressionless guards—all women, all blond, all silent—check the passports of a populace still sleepy and in its underwear. The impression is that nothing can surprise them.

I can't seem to get to sleep. The train is running over a dark land, past infrequent lights and distant farms. Looking at a map, boarding a train, crossing a continent: childish, isn't it? But every so often adults need to do childish things, and railway fantasies, let's admit it, aren't the most dangerous kind. Trains are places of exchange, study, and rest. You don't need to rush toward the world; it's the world that rushes toward you.

Trains are generators of meetings and farewells. They are concert halls—all you need is a pair of earbuds—and reading groups. They are a classic idea, impervious to fashion, just like bicycles and watches and clocks with hands and a dial. They are cradles and cozy nooks, places for meditation, and gymnasiums for the imagination. Where do they go, those silent women who tuck their light coats around them to ward off prying eyes and the wind? What do those young people have in mind as they lean against the restroom door and chat? What's going on, in this ordinary night in Eastern Europe, that we don't know now and never will?

> *Lend me your great noise, your great smooth speed,*
> *Your nocturnal gliding across lighted Europe.*

These lines were written by the Frenchman Valery Larbaud, an eccentric individual who was also known under the pseudonyms A. O. Barnabooth, L. Hagiosy, and X. M. Tourmier de Zamble. His father owned the company that bottled Vichy mineral water, and he traveled in luxury toward the end of the belle époque; he was troubled by some lingering sense of guilt, but on the whole he enjoyed himself. Things are different now: Ukrainian trains aren't luxurious and the epoch we live in isn't particularly lovely. Still, rolling by night across a brightly lighted Europe is a profoundly stirring thing. You need only wait for your heartbeat to catch the rhythm of the train, and hope that Mark doesn't fall off the ladder to the upper bunk again.

In Kraków

From Kraków station, just outside of the Old Town, we go straight to the Italian Cultural Institute. We find a small crowd curious to gawk at four vagabonds, and we slip into several interesting discussions of railway philosophy.

The first one concerns Karol Wojtyła, this city's former archbishop and adopted son. John Paul II looms over the Market Square, the largest medieval square in Europe: he appears on billboards, posters, banners. How important was he to the defeat of Communism? Maybe not as important as they believe in Poland and more important than they believe in America.

The second discussion has to do with the ideal train trip. We discover that the wildest dreams of those present range from the Orient Express to the Trans-Siberian Express, from a trip as a couple to Chongqing, China, to a dinner in the restaurant car with Mark Spörrle. The dining companion in question feigns modesty, but he doesn't rule it out entirely.

The third discussion has to do with the cardinal points of the compass. Stephan Bielanski, a professor at the Jagiellonian University, inquires, "In Italy, why do you include Poland among the Eastern European countries when we're right in the center of Europe? You only need to glance at a map."

I reply: You need to start from Germany, which is at the very center of Europe. Not the geographic center, but the economic, political, and psychological center. It's the richest, most populous, and most influential country in the European Union. Having established that it's the center, everything else follows naturally. There is a north (Scandinavia, the British Isles), a south (the Mediterranean countries), and a west (from France to Portugal). The east, for the Europeans, begins at the river Oder. Is Vienna east of Prague? True, it is, but that doesn't matter. In some cases, history, economics, and psychology count more than geography does.

At this point, we stop discussing trains and longitude and we head for the buffet, which is excellent and well organized. Usually I hate buffets—they bring out the worst in mankind—but this one is an exception. Daria comes up to me, announces that she is one of my readers, and says: "I want to give you a book." I turn pale. Giving a book to a traveler is an act of cruelty. It will be a deadweight in his suitcase for many days to come (unless the recipient abandons the book in his hotel room, which is something I've learned to do without turning a hair).

How wrong I was! Thank you, Daria. Not only is the book light and convenient; it's titled *How to Write Like Chekhov: Advice and Inspiration, Straight from His Own Letters and Work*. The editor starts from Anton Chekhov's travel memoir *The Island of Sakhalin*, a piece of reporting from the easternmost corner of the czarist empire, and extrapolates advice for those setting out on long journeys and who are interested in telling the tale.

I leaf through the book and discover a number of intelligent suggestions:

Talk Things Over with Friends

Challenge Indifference

Read and Summarize

Be Ready to Revise Your Opinions

Do Not Make Too Many Plans

Count, Measure, Weigh

Make Inventories

Walk in Company

Stroll Alone

Observe by Day and by Night

Use All Five Senses

Collect Facts

Read the Local Papers

And his last, most magnificent advice of all:

Accept Invitations

Gentle readers of Kraków! Who wants four talkative and ravenous travelers en route to Prague as dinner guests? They'll tell you all about Anton Chekhov and the Polish railways.

Arriving in Prague

Have you heard of Prakrapest? It's a legendary city. A place long beloved of the Italians, who are drawn here by excellent beer, old houses by the river, and beautiful young women. It's at once exotic and familiar, mysterious and welcoming, comprehensible and indecipherable. Having progressed from dictatorship to democracy, and from terrible cooking to boring cuisine, Prakrapest is crisscrossed by quivers of capitalist economy and swarms of students. Only in the times of the USSR were the throngs so numerous, and those were throngs of secret agents.

Prakrapest! A portmanteau word made up of Prague (where we are now), Kraków (where we were before), and Budapest (where we shall not go). A city that, in the minds of many tourists, overlaps, melds, and gets confused. The Italian equivalent, for the Americans, would be Rovenence (Rome + Venice + Florence). After a week, you can't tell one church from another, and the special tourist menus all look alike.

What about the Germans? Do they love Prague? One of them, who lives here, tells me, "A lukewarm, respectful love, bordering on apathy. The Czech Republic is a well-mannered neighbor who never makes noise: we just don't think about them." This crucible of a city, which fused together the best of the Slavic soul, the Germanic influence, and the Jewish tradition, no longer exerts the allure it once did. The tourists from Hamburg prefer the Costa del Sol, and visiting German politicians don't even bother to stay the night.

Prague! I first arrived here in 1982 by motorcycle, on my way from Budapest and heading for Kraków. I came back in 1988 and again in 1989, a young foreign correspondent, and for two months I covered the "Velvet Revolution," which deposed the grim and obtuse Communist regime. It was a special city that winter: Václavské Náměstí (Wenceslas Square) was full of police and hope, with cautious conversations at the Café Slavia, at the far end of the Národní, overlooking the Moldau River. There was no Internet; there were no cell phones. And yet back then we felt we understood things, perhaps because we had plenty of time to watch, to talk, and to think.

Václav Klaus, who later became president of the Czech Republic, used to cut his calling cards out of a sheet of xeroxed paper, using a pair of nail scissors. Václav Havel, a dissident playwright, welcomed people into his book-lined home. Just months later, when he became president, he invited me to the Castle and explained something important to me: dictatorships are filthy and disgusting, but they produce good literature. "And that is why even I, who suffered under the dictatorship and spent time in prison, run the risk of feeling a certain nostalgia for it," he said with a note of concern in his voice.

I've come back other times, in different seasons, both political and meteorological. The city is always sumptuous, but it's a stage awaiting a performance. That performance could arrive any second; there's no saying. The young women of Prague—the Agnezkas and Dorotas who are waiting for the bus this evening, while they look at their phones— would ask me: "Velvet Revolution? Is that an advertisement for a new skin cream?"

On to Vienna

Departure for Vienna. Appointment at 7:45 a.m. at Praha Hlavní, Prague's central train station, inaugurated in 1871 by Emperor Franz Joseph. The current art nouveau station was built between 1901 and 1909 to plans by the Czech architect Josef Fanta (no relation to the orange soda of the same name). During the First Czechoslovak Republic, the station was called Wilson Station, in honor of the president of the United States of America Woodrow Wilson. Then the pro-Soviet Communists, to no one's surprise, changed the name.

Everything unfolds according to script: Soledad and Gianni are right on time, I get there at the last minute, and Mark is late. The taxi driver looks like one of the Blues Brothers, he's driving an old French sedan, he wants to speak Italian, and he's listening to syncopated Tyrolean music: in Bohemia, a difficult assortment to metabolize first thing in the morning. And that's not all. In Prague station, the tracks are indicated with a letter according to the cardinal points of the compass. But watch it: *S* doesn't indicate the tracks on the south side of the station, but the ones on the north (*sever* in Czech).

Miraculously, we find the Franz Schubert train no. 75, departing at 8:39 a.m., and we board car 262. A hostess offers us beverages and newspapers, but only in the local language. She's a cherub standing almost six feet tall, smiling but impassive. If Mark and I jumped up and started doing the Hully Gully on our seats—which we exclude from the outset, far too much effort required—the young woman would ask: "Tea or coffee?"

Bohemia rolls past us, verdant. I'm eager to see whether at the border with Austria—which I crossed years ago by car—there are still armies of garden gnomes, one of the specialties of the place's craftsmen, which attract aficionados (or are they maniacs?) from various countries. No garden gnomes this time. But a good friend, who lives in Vienna, has promised to greet us with one when we arrive.

It's a day of strange presences. As we approach the Austrian capital, each of us wrapped in his or her own electronic microcosm (Mark writes; Soledad translates; Gianni edits videos; I listen to Tom Waits), a little yellow chick appears. You read that right: it's a plush toy—it doesn't peep, but it's certainly a little yellow chick. Where has it been until now? Don't ask me. Herr Spörrle makes the introductions: *das Küken*. His daughter gave it to him, asking him to take pictures of it during his trip. We immediately realize that we won't be rid of it till we get to Lisbon.

Vienna greets us with dazzling sunshine and crystal clear air: if it weren't for the difference in architecture, traffic, and GDP, it would seem as if we were in Tunis. We do a public opinion survey, video camera in hand, among the Viennese populace, asking whom they prefer, Italians or Germans (all things considered, they prefer Italians—just saying!). Over the course of the day, the little yellow chick will make appearances in a vending machine, inside a green plant, and stretched out on an elephant tusk. Thanks, Mark. This trip is becoming increasingly interesting.

From Vienna to Zurich

In the middle of the journey, and on the eve of this stretch through the mountains, we need to take care of a few matters. For starters, the issue of punctuality. Mark and I are accused of always showing up late for departure, but that's not fair. I admit that our entrances in the various train stations are always hasty and last-minute, but whose fault is it that the Viennese taxi driver had a trunk full of spray paint cans and couldn't fit our luggage in? Are we seriously being blamed for the troops of tourists who always seem to be directly in our way?

Anyway, here we are. An imperially sunny morning and the Vienna–Zurich train no. 162 departing at 9:14 a.m. entirely lives up to our expectations. Full of light, comfortable, probably the cleanest train in Europe. One screen shows the itinerary of the trip (Linz, Salzburg, Innsbruck, Sankt Anton am Arlberg, then Switzerland). There are three classes of seating: two first classes and one second class (don't ask me why). The average age of the passengers is that of Jimmy Carter. An attendant passes by with an onion omelet that, first thing in the morning, constitutes a chemical weapon.

By now, Mark's little yellow chick is a member of the group. It appeared on its chaperone's shoulder at breakfast. I responded with a garden gnome, given me by a reader. But the garden gnome was left behind in Vienna. The little yellow chick stalks us, implacable.

Since we are midway through our journey—both in time and in distance: seven days out of fourteen, 1,986 miles out of 3,930—here are our Oscars of the First Week.

Best Hotel: Das Triest, Vienna (we were ecstatic)

Worst Hotel: Élite, Prague (we fled)

Best Restaurant: Kvartira 44, Moscow (memorable herrings)

Worst Restaurant: Hotel Metropol, Moscow (Soviet-era service)

Best Buffet: Italian Cultural Institute, Kraków

Cleanest Restroom: Vienna–Zurich train (absolutely inhuman in its cleanliness)

Most Demanding Leg of the Trip: nocturnal journey from Kiev to Kraków

Most Idyllic Leg of the Trip: Salzburg–Innsbruck–Sankt Anton (the grazing horses work for the tourism board)

Most Beautiful Square: Red Square, Moscow, by night

Most Baffling Station: Kraków, where the underpasses all have women's names (and are closed)

Most Literary Station: Kiyevskaya Station, in Moscow (you expect to see Turgenev selling beverages)

City I Was Sorriest to Leave: Prague

Best Line of the Week: "I'm wearing jeans" (Igor, our Ukrainian translator, on how to find him in the Kiev station, where EVERY-ONE wears jeans).

From Zurich to Lyon, via Geneva

Zurich has chosen to greet us with an unusual heat—eighty-five degrees—that allows the city's residents to indulge in their Mediterranean fantasies. Last night, it was quite a show: people were stripping down, walking around barefoot, playing chess by the lake, listening to fake-Latin music sitting in fake-Italian bistros, in little fake-seaside piazzas. Staggering like sailors newly returned to dry land (eight days aboard a train takes its toll), we wound up at the restaurant Pulcino (of course, that's Italian for "little yellow chick"!), where the Russian waitress and the Egyptian maître d' were doing their best to seem, respectively, Ligurian and Pugliese.

For once, Mark and I got to the station early. Waiting for us is an editor at the *Neue Zürcher Zeitung* (*NZZ*) for an interview. We talk about our horizontal Europe and we venture various railway allegories. With reference to the two classes of travel (by now we're capable only of binary track thinking), I explain, "If Austria and Germany are in first class, economically speaking, Italy is in the (noisy) passageway between first and second class. And Switzerland is better than anyone: premium class."

The train departs, and we realize immediately: this isn't a train. It's a self-powered penthouse. Intercity no. 718, consisting of two-story carriages with panoramic vistas, rolls gently along from Zurich to Bern, and then beyond, toward Lausanne and Geneva, as if it were reluctant to disturb the quiet of the Helvetian Sunday morning. The mountains seem to part, good-naturedly, to let us pass. The meadows glitter. Grazing cattle bob their heads in a sign of approval. It's all unquestionably very beautiful: it seems like we've slipped into the packaging of a chocolate bar.

We cross the border between Switzerland and France and enter Latin Europe, which we won't leave until we reach Lisbon. We change trains. In France the expressions change; the colors change; the sounds change; the shared concept of cleanliness and order changes. In our tiny double-decker car—we've moved from a penthouse to a studio apartment—our world has suddenly become much less homogeneous. We're riding with Arabs, Asians, Africans; miniskirts mix with designer suits and tracksuits worn proudly by overweight white males. The Sunday sunshine roars over the French roofs, and people in their backyards watch the train go by, completely unaware of the unusual foursome riding along inside (plus the little yellow chick).

At 3:21 p.m., right on schedule, we arrive in Lyon's Part-Dieu station. Lots of policemen, people out strolling, bicycles, and sweat. The female train attendants get out with us, wearing tight-fitting pink sleeveless shirts. A young couple, curious about the video camera, ask us where we come from: one of us is German, three are Italians, and the little yellow chick is stateless, we reply.

Lyon is the third-largest city in France, founded by a lieutenant of

Julius Caesar's at Cicero's suggestion. Today it is a manufacturing center, producing machine tools and offering health services, and it has a sumptuous historical center: twelve hundred acres classified by UNESCO as a World Heritage site, the largest area after Venice. *"Avant, avant, Lion le melhor!"* reads the city's motto, in Arpitan. It means "Forward, forward, Lyon is the best," of course. Obviously for us Italians. Not for Mark, who had his moment of glory between Vienna and Zurich—where he had home-field advantage—and from now on, he'll need our help. All right, we'll help him. We'll even tell him what "Arpitan" means, if he'll cut it out with the little yellow chick.

From Lyon to Marseille

The lady in red looks at us with dislike, which is promptly returned. Then she exchanges a few conspiratorial glances with her husband—a corpulent fellow, with thick, snowy hair and the sadness of someone who remembers he was once a handsome man—but fails to notice that I'm watching them. For starters, he had said, in a vinegary tone: "I don't like video cameras." As if Gianni, given the opportunity to film Mark with his yellow chick, had time to waste on the two of them.

In Lyon, a summer sun is shining. We take the TGV leaving for Nice at 2:37 p.m., but we'll stop at Marseille. It must be the heat, but we've been treated rudely more frequently on this leg of the journey than in the entire trip from Moscow. The taxi driver in Lyon flew into a rage because I tried to remove the luggage from the trunk, without waiting for him to do it. A policeman warned us not to film in the station. Aboard the train, a young couple has taken our seats, and they show no intention of moving. To justify his refusal, the young man—who vaguely resembles Mark's little yellow chick, only fatter—pulls out the Syllogism of the Obtuse Traveler: "Someone else took our seats, so we took these. Why don't you go complain to the people who took our seats?"

I explain to him, with a smile and my very best French, that that's not the way things work. These are our seats, the train is full, and most important of all, we need to work. I add a geographic reference, to play on his empathy: "We've been traveling for eight days; we started in Moscow." And he replies, austerely: "I don't give a damn where you come from." Well, that's no way to reply to salty old wolves of the rails like us. I assign the case to Soledad, who can't wait to launch into a multilingual attack: five minutes later, our seats are free and ready for us. *"Bon voyage,"* I whisper to the usurper as he retreats in the face of a stern conductor. *"Vous aussi,"* he replies. His companion glares daggers at him, clearly seething: "You helpless rabbit!"

Experienced travelers know, however, you shouldn't overemphasize a single episode and draw larger general conclusions from it. Our twenty-four hours in Lyon brought us examples of true courtesy and genuine surprises. We walked and walked, happy to stretch our lower limbs (our upper limbs are in fine shape, chiefly because of the constant lifting and lowering of our luggage). We saw a great many things. Les Halles de Lyon Paul Bocuse, a temple to gastronomy! Croix-Rousse, the neighborhood of the old-fashioned silk workers (roller shutters lowered)! Brasserie Le Sud, nominated for the Best Restaurant of the Second Week! In the afternoon, on a bridge, we philosophized about the importance of the light sweater in the tourist aesthetic.

We depart again, happy to be back on the train. By now, we're clinical cases. Dromomania was the diagnosis of a reader who is a psychiatrist: an obsession with wandering, going places, getting on the road. Dromomania! If that's true, I wouldn't really mind. After all, this anxiety took us from Russia to southern France, where tonight we can hope to see the sea appear unexpectedly, as we round a curve. It doesn't happen. But at the station of Marseille Saint-Charles, the wind brings us the smell of salt water, and that is enough for us.

From Marseille to Barcelona, via Montpellier

A boat! This is Mark's latest brilliant idea. Herr Spörrle says: we're always on the train (true), ten days is a long time (correct), Marseille and Barcelona face each other over the same stretch of sea (undeniable). But what boat captain would take four people like us aboard (to say nothing of the little yellow chick)? We walk down to the old harbor. Just as a joke, we ask the sailors on a gigantic yacht if they'll give us a ride. When we ask them, "Can we get to Barcelona with this yacht?" they immediately burst into enthusiasm. The captain, they explain, lives in Palma de Mallorca, and would be only too happy to turn his prow westward. The captain in question joins us on dry land—early forties, bearded, with a movie star face—and tells us the price: twelve thousand euros a day, crew and fuel are extra.

Fishing boats, catamarans, sailboats, regatta racers, large rubber dinghies: no one else wants to take us seriously. It's not the end of the world. We climb aboard a little tourist minitrain—our karma always brings us to this—and we devote ourselves to the exploration of the Panier, the old fishermen's quarter, recently gentrified. Boarding with us is a class of French schoolchildren. The children study us, and they seem to consider us exotic. And how can we disagree? An Italian and a German who are speaking English in France, and the taller of the two carries a little yellow chick with him everywhere he goes.

Marseille doesn't have much of a reputation, but it's actually an interesting city. World famous for an anthem, a soap, and a harbor and its traditional organized crime, the city proves to be full of life and passion. The hotel—with a spectacular view of the old port, an imperial bed, and a metaphysical shower—allows us to check out late, and we sit for a few hours reading outdoors. "Work, work, work . . . I prefer the sound of the sea." Poet Dino Campana—even though he was referring to a different sea—understood it all.

The taxi takes us to the station, slaloming past multicolored pedestrians who simply can't be persuaded to respect the traffic lights. Train for Bordeaux departing at 4:12 p.m., but we're getting out at Montpellier. An hour's wait there for the connecting train. We should reach Barcelona—our third-to-last stop on this trip—at 10:45 that night. According to the Catalonian time zone, just in time for dinner.

In Barcelona

I'm in a hotel in Barcelona that seems like a karaoke of Taipei, with interior decoration by the cousins of Dolce & Gabbana on behalf of a soccer player: purple leather and silver picture frames, a black bathroom and gold pillows, leopard-skin blankets. We've just returned from a morning out bicycling.

Under an enameled sky—a blue lid over the Rambla—I tot up the accounts of our journey, which began in Moscow and has Lisbon as its destination. So far, two weeks, nine countries, eleven cities, 3,977 miles. Today, May 9, is Europe Day; but, as usual, no one has noticed. And yet, there's plenty to celebrate. I wouldn't want to seem romantic and naive to you—better than cynical and resigned, in any case—but I assure you: Europe exists. These recent days have confirmed what I've seen in thirty years of journalism and travel. Changing every night— four Slavic languages, then two cities in German, then two French cities, and now two Spanish ones, all the while speaking English, as well—pushes the brain to seek out common denominators. You become a foreigner right at home. It's a good exercise, and every European ought to try it out from time to time.

Europe exists and it resembles itself. So we don't have a common foreign policy and security policy? That's true, and it's a mistake. Was the introduction of the euro—without bothering to unify our tax and budget policies—a less-than-perfect operation? It certainly was. But the common currency, the cell phones that ring everywhere, the mixed, understandable languages, the populist right wings and the slovenly left wings, the train stations illuminated by night, the police all with the same gazes, none too stern, the bars and cafés and menus, the students who feel at home wherever they go, the great cathedrals built by great sinners: all this reminds the traveler that there really is such a thing as Europe.

Kraków isn't Barcelona and it isn't Zurich. Still, it more closely resembles Barcelona and Zurich than it does Phoenix or Rio de Janeiro. Any American, Chinese, Japanese, or South African will tell you this is true. But since we live in the midst of the forest—a very nice forest indeed—we're unable to see it. All we can see are the trunks of the trees, and every once in a while we bang our heads against them.

The migrants have a point. They consider Europe a safe and welcoming place: it's not the same thing to raise a family in Benghazi as in Barcelona. The more tragedies occur in Africa and in the Middle East, the more the European Union will appear in the eyes of those people as exactly what it is: a haven in a storm, built by a generation that lived through a hurricane. It took decades of dictatorships (Communism, Nazism, Fascism) and two world wars, but our parents understood: Europe at peace is a masterpiece and it needs to be treated with a gentle touch.

Could someone explain that to the racists, please? Actually, I have an even better idea: take the racists and put them on a train and convince them to cross a continent that remains an island of good sense in the larger, unreasonable sea of the rest of the world. Let me repeat: the new arrivals sense this; our ancestors knew it. We are less intelligent, but we are capable of learning. If so, we can teach these things to our children, who need to hear them.

From Barcelona to Madrid

Trains are ritualistic places. After two weeks I know my own habits and I recognize those of my traveling companions.

Gianni puts on his earphones and reviews the material filmed during that day's travel; when he smiles, it means that Mark has really given the best of himself. Every once in a while, Gianni will notice something: the indication of the train's speed (between Barcelona and Madrid we hit 301 kilometers per hour, which is 187 miles per hour); an amusing and unexpected development; a particularly eccentric passenger. In those cases, he'll pull out one of his video cameras—he has three: a small one, a medium one, and a big one—he'll leap to his feet, and he'll start filming. At that point a conductor will arrive and inform him that, in trains and at stations, filming is forbidden. He'll smile and say: "No problem." Because he's already done filming.

Soledad prefers the window seat, even if she doesn't look out much: she has too much translating to do. When she works, she puts her hair up and gets down to it, periodically murmuring comments in all the languages of the United Nations. If you ask her something, she raises her head and gazes at you with a pair of distracted blue eyes. You might announce that you just saw an ichthyosaurus go by, emblazoned with the logo of the Goethe-Institut, and she'd reply, "Ah. How nice."

Mark observes, records, and comments upon every detail of the train we're traveling in. He describes particularities, criticizes shortcomings, lauds the conveniences. Yesterday between Barcelona and Madrid—as we sped across Aragon into the setting sun—Herr Spörrle was praising the high level of service, superior to what is found in Germany: hot wet napkins, newspapers, spumante, orange juice, and mineral water (still or bubbly). In the *servicio de bebidas*—presented by a platinum-haired attendant, an Iberian Ivana Trump—there was also Martini Rojo and the D.O. Ribera del Duero Señorio de Nava *vino tinto*. I didn't taste it myself, but I have to admit that it has a magnificent name.

Then there's me. In comparison with my traveling companions, I spend less time on my computer and more time just watching: the landscape outside, the people inside. I like to read: books and trains are natural lovers. I don't think there necessarily has to be a direct relationship between places and titles: here in Spain, it's not mandatory to read

Javier Marías or Carlos Ruiz Zafón. In a great novel, after all, there's always everything. In the past few days I've been reading Dostoevsky's *The Idiot*, which I brought with me from Moscow and which I'd like to finish before reaching Lisbon. During his lengthy nocturnal exposition, young Ippolit says something that I find fascinating:

> On the other hand, all your thoughts, all the seeds scattered by you, perhaps forgotten by you, will grow up and take form. He who has received them from you will hand them on to another. And how can you tell what part you may have in the future determination of the destinies of humanity?

You can understand that it's tough to travel with this burden of responsibility on our shoulders. What if someone chose to imitate us, retracing our itinerary? And then what if that person fell in love with a Polish co-ed or a Swiss business lawyer and decided to move across the continent or the world? Anything can happen on a long train journey! I'll need to talk to the others about it, later, on the night train for Lisbon. Far ahead, down that track—we can't see it, but we can already sense it—the ocean awaits us, the ocean, across which no one has ever yet laid tracks. Not even the Germans, though they know how to do anything.

From Madrid to Lisbon

The evening in Madrid, the last evening of our trip, is relaxed. Light drizzle and a holiday feel in the air, with the help of the Festival of Saint Isidore. After some hesitation, we dine in the little Taberna Embroque on Calle de Recoletos, a gathering spot for aficionados of the corrida. On the television, live coverage from the *plaza de toros*, and Soledad—surrounded by autographed photographs of *toreros*—is forced to stifle her animal rights instincts. On the photo of the legendary Juan

Belmonte is written: *"Se torea, como se es"* (literally, "you fight the bulls the way you are"). Replace the Spanish verb *torear* with the Spanish verb *viajar*: here, too, you can't bluff.

Trains are like boats, like camping, like prison. After fifteen days together, twenty-four hours a day, either you put up with one another or you strangle one another. Mark, Sole, Gianni, and I have developed our little tics, and we get along well. I understood it a few days ago as we were boarding a taxi: each of us knows exactly where to fit in and what to do, as if we were hopping onto a four-man bobsled. Tonight, too, as we head for the Madrid Chamartín station, we move with perfect coordination. Sole has the tickets; Gianni has his plans; Mark has his silences; I have my fantasies.

The night train for Lisbon leaves from Track 14 at 10:25 p.m. It's clean and tidy, with a deserted and very literary dining car, almost elegant. The walls are pink plastic, and they produce a certain Barbie Dreamhouse effect. We're welcomed by a courteous Portuguese conductor, who asks, "Do you have permits to film?" I reply, "We don't have them and we never have, all the way from Moscow. So please don't ruin everything now." He smiles and says, "All right," and turns to go. Then we drink cold Mateus wine, as the Europe available to us dwindles. Behind us lies a continent, and this evening it's starting to weigh on us.

OSCARS FOR THE SECOND WEEK

Best Bathroom: Sofitel Vieux Port, Marseille (tropical shower with view of the harbor)

Best Bed: Hospes Puerta de Alcalá, Madrid (all four of us could have slept in one bed)

Worst Wi-Fi: Hospes Puerta de Alcalá, Madrid (at the reception desk they wouldn't know a wireless network from a fisherman's net)

Best Restaurant: Brasserie Le Sud, Lyon (exquisite, on the banks of the Rhône, and not even particularly expensive)

Worst Restaurant: Pulcino, Zurich (everything was modest, except for the price)

Most Disagreeable Encounter: the usurpers of our reserved seats on the Lyon–Marseille TGV

Most Agreeable Encounter: the young woman in Montpellier who blew us a kiss as the train pulled out

The Chicest Leg of the Trip: the high-speed train from Barcelona to Madrid

The Most Comfortable Leg of the Trip: train from Zurich to Geneva

The Most Spectacular Leg: Montpellier–Figueres (water all around, big sky)

Most Comfortable Sleeping Compartment: Madrid–Lisbon

Most Mysterious Station: Marseille

Station Most Closely Resembling an Airport: Barcelona Sants

Most Elegant Station: Madrid Atocha

Most Surprising City: Lyon

City We Were Sorriest to Leave: Lisbon, because it meant the end of the trip

Line of the Week: "The tall one is my wife; the short one is my daughter" (Mark, showing us a photograph of his wife and four-year-old daughter).

In Lisbon

With the early sun behind us and the last stretch of the river Tagus ahead of us, the train stops at Lisbon Santa Apólonia station: there's no more land to run on.

The morning glitters like a majolica tile; the air is still. We've arrived. Moscow seems far away but within reach. Only overland travel makes it possible to understand distances and metabolize changes. Planes conveniently move our bodies from one place to another, but our brains don't follow.

I find that I'm not as excited as I'd imagined. A little tired, instead, in part because I haven't gotten much sleep. The freight trains of Estremadura province are noisy, and by night the stations of the Lusitania are too alluring to resist gazing out at. I stop, wheeled suitcase in one hand and backpack slung over my shoulders, on the platform in front of the train. I imagine that the look on my face must be that of an astronaut as he leaves the spacecraft, but it doesn't matter. We've arrived, and no arrival should ever be taken for granted.

Gianni has been up since dawn, and he's shooting, recording, archiving, and planning.

Mark has taken advantage of the breakfast (included) and now he's looking around: it's never too early for an inspection tour.

At the station we meet Susanne Höhn, director of the Goethe-Institut, who has flown here from Rome, and her colleague Joachim, from the Goethe-Institut of Lisbon. I had asked her to pick up fifteen red roses for Soledad. One for each day of the trip, one for each job she was forced to take on: interpreter, translator, organizer, treasurer, travel agent, tour guide, tech consultant, bodyguard, secret agent, polemicist, therapist, moderator, cultural mediator, arbiter, and woman. A calling that sums them all up, on trains and off.

4

From Sydney to Perth:
The Indian Pacific

> Trains, for instance. He wasn't a child anymore
> and it wasn't the machinery that fascinated him.
> If he preferred night trains, it was because they
> struck him as somehow strange, a little sordid.
>
> **GEORGES SIMENON,**
> *THE MAN WHO WATCHED THE TRAINS GO BY*

This story was written in a notebook received as a gift in Mantua, with a ballpoint pen pilfered in Melbourne, under the eyes of eight Australian retirees, in the presence of a double for Bill Clinton, while surrounded by emus, eagles, and kangaroos. Here I should be specific, because you see a great many kangaroos aboard the Indian Pacific. Many of them are stylized, reproduced, emblazoned on doors, menus, and napkins. Others, real but dead, along the tracks; a few living ones, glimpsed in the distance, with that stunned expression that you will find only on the face of a kangaroo at the sight of a train (or on the face of an Italian member of parliament who's been caught with an offshore bank account).

So, how does an ostensibly normal fifty-year-old make plans and reservations, move heaven and earth, struggle, argue, and fly around the world to board a train that then proceeds to travel in an almost unvaryingly straight line? The trip, 2,704 miles, lasts three days and three nights. The departure is from Sydney on Saturday; the arrival is in Perth on Tuesday. Average speed of fifty-three miles per hour, hitting high points of seventy miles per hour. The most exciting stretch is the Nullarbor Plain, crossed by the longest straightaway of rail track in the world (297 miles). "Nullarbor" comes from the Latin and it means "no trees." Let's say that it's a precise, laconic, and optimistic description.

But nothingness has its allure for an Italian who comes from the land of too much.

Saturday, First Day

Tourist offices, travel agencies, and young ladies on the phone had assured me that there was no room on the train as far as Perth; at Adelaide, I was going to have to catch a plane. But Italian travelers don't argue; they simply remain skeptical. They don't complain; they investigate. At Sydney Central Station I ask: "Is there room?" Answer: "We've just had a cancellation. There's a place available in Red Kangaroo." Unaware of the chromatic implications of the marsupials in question, I reply, "I'll take it."

I discover that Red Kangaroo means second class. No problem: the Indian Pacific is one of the great railway journeys on the planet. The line was built to persuade the colonies of Western Australia to join the federation. Inaugurated in 1917, it had been constructed in five years using picks, shovels, carts, and camels. There remained the problem of the different gauges: to go from Sydney to Perth, you had to change trains six times. I only have to change my sleeping compartment in Adelaide. That seems doable.

//////////////////

Boarding an old train is a ceremony full of joy and apprehension, like boarding a new boat. Tonight, and only for tonight, I'm a guest in Gold Kangaroo, the first class. The sleeping compartment is wood paneled, with two bunks perpendicular to the tracks. I see a tiny bathroom, with a shower designed for Smurfs. Everywhere are secret caches, cubbyholes, and curious mechanisms. At 2:55 p.m., as I'm studying the retractable sink, the train moves. At 3:05 it suddenly brakes, and I bang my shin against the open door. That's my fault: I should have followed the Train Safe recommendations published in the onboard magazine, and done my exercises. ("Push your bottom backward against your seat. Raise one butt cheek. Repeat three times per side.")

After an hour I move into the lounge car, currently occupied by a group of retirees from Bega, New South Wales. They aren't looking out the window at the Blue Mountains. They're busy applauding the conductor as he explains life aboard the train. The man resembles Bill Clinton, and he knows it. Like the former president, he loves to seduce his audience. He explains that the sign DRESS CODES APPLY basically means "flip-flops prohibited." Apparently, at least one person has lost a big toe while moving from one carriage to another.

I continue my explorations. I walk through restaurant cars, galleys, baggage cars, second class (I mean Red Kangaroo, where I'll fetch up tomorrow). Toward the end of the train—isolated, magnificent, and empty—is the Vice Royal Lounge Car, the carriage that carried the representative of the British Crown during the opening ceremonies of the Trans-Australian Railway. I am informed that it is used only on special occasions. On this trip, it's empty and off-limits. I smile and make a mental note for later.

I return to Gold Kangaroo, among the giddy retirees from New South Wales. Some of them know all about trains, and they trade esoteric books. Their driver-companion is called Malcom, and he invites me to his table for dinner. He's fifty years old, and he resembles the eldest Dalton brother: tall, gangly, lantern jaw, a fiercely amiable grin. This evening he's decided he needs to tend to my railway education. "Until recently," he explains, "off-road cars and trail bikes could ride along next to the tracks. But every time a vehicle broke down, the driver would flag down the Indian Pacific to avoid roasting to death in the outback. So it's now illegal to ride along the tracks."

Also sharing our table are Bill—Australian, seventy years old, he went to school with the former prime minister John Howard—and Carl, English, forty. He was let go by the pharmaceutical company where he worked: with his severance pay he decided to do some traveling. He tells us about his teenage son who's obsessed with opals and explains the difference between singlet, doublet, and triplet opals. The cook, who's from Liverpool, comes to say hello. We drink Shiraz wine and set our watches ahead by thirty minutes. Malcom/Dalton tells me: "You and I are the same. Bus drivers and travel writers work on holiday." I say good night and retire to my compartment. I'll have something to think about in my bunk.

Sunday, Second Day

There's a sadistic streak in conductors. At 6:10 a.m. Clinton's look-alike announces that at 6:30 he'll announce breakfast service, first and second shifts (6:45 and 7:15). He uses a distinctly emphatic English: "Breakfast will commence," he says. Then he informs us that passengers will be able to detrain (get out, I translate to myself) at Broken Hill, again in two shifts. The Indian Pacific—twenty-five cars, two locomotives, 2,255 feet long—is too long for the little platform.

It isn't easy to follow this line of thought at dawn, but Broken Hill is worth it: Australia's longest-running mining town, in the middle of nowhere, in the far west of outback New South Wales. If only we could go and see it. The tour of the city has been canceled, but from the train we see straight streets, the legacy of miners and gamblers. Many Italians came here to work, over the course of the twentieth century. Even more went to Adelaide, three hundred miles away, where we arrive at 3 p.m. and depart at 6:40 p.m. I go for a quick sightseeing tour of the city, meet the Italian consul, drink a beer with some of my local readers, and make a discovery. There are 120 Italian regional clubs in Australia, 25 of which have their own offices. Italians love Italy, when they are far away.

Adelaide brings back memories. In 1983, when I first visited Australia, I was twenty-six. My first assignment as a foreign correspondent, actually. The day before my flight back to Europe, I met a girl from Växjö, Sweden—Annica was her name—and I fell madly in love, canceled my flight, and from here—Adelaide, South Australia—I sent a telegram to my editor in chief (no e-mail, back then). "Missing in action. Everything's great. See you in a month." He should have fired me, but he didn't. When I finally got back, he told me: "Jumping ship while away on your first assignment! You are nuts. Good. You need to be a little crazy to be a good journalist. Welcome back."

I get back aboard, and the train pulls out again. The retirees from New South Wales are excited. The Indian Pacific shakes them from side to side as if they were dolls, but it's almost time for drinks and then dinner; their children are far away: what more could they ask for? While the train approaches the lights of Port Augusta—the last supermarket before Alice Springs, in the middle of Australia—Malcom/ Dalton asks the attendant where she comes from. Her name is Gabrielle. She sits down with us and smiles the way only nurses, kindergarten teachers, and young women on trains know how to do. "Norfolk Island," she replies. He says: "Norfolk Island? They called it the 'Inferno in the Pacific'! That's where they sent the worst criminals. The present-day inhabitants are their descendants." Gabrielle stops smiling, stands up, and walks away. Malcom admits that he often seems to say the wrong thing to girls.

Night in Red Kangaroo. Shared bathroom. The corridor, narrow and undulating, necessarily becomes an alternating one-way passageway. The bunk runs parallel to the rails, allowing you to fall asleep while looking out at the South Australia desert as it streams past. We second-class passengers know how to settle for what we get.

Monday, Third Day

In the southern darkness, the Indian Pacific has passed through Boo-kaloo, Wirraminna, Kultanaby, and Kingoonya: places that might be of interest to new parents, who are always in search of original names for their kids. At dawn we pull into Tarcoola, founded by gold prospectors in 1901. The place once had two thousand inhabitants; now it has two, but it still remains the meeting point between the Indian Pacific (east–west, Perth–Sydney) and the Ghan (north–south, Darwin–Adelaide).

We enter the Nullarbor, the straightaway of straightaways. We pass Ooldea; twenty miles to the north is Maralinga, where the English tested their atom bombs from 1956 to 1963, after evicting the Aboriginals. A short while later, we stop at Cook. We get out to take pictures of the signs. My favorites: OUR HOSPITAL NEEDS YOUR HELP: GET SICK and IF YOU'RE A CROOK / COME TO COOK. But not even crooks want to live here. Officially, Cook has a population of four, but no one is in sight. Probably they're hiding so we can't take their pictures.

On the ground I find a screw as big as a bottle, and I take it as a souvenir (if I forget to remove it from my carry-on luggage at the airport, I'll be arrested). The train pulls out again. I head for the next-to-last carriage, the exclusive and off-limits Vice Royal Lounge Car. I get comfortable in one of the seats and for two hours I look out at the red earth, the blue sky, and the big wedge-tailed eagles that climb to six thousand feet, ignoring the train of which they are the emblem. Every so often someone in uniform comes by and courteously asks me what I'm doing there. I smile and reply: "I'm Italian." The explanation always seems to work, so I remain to admire the sunset over the Nullarbor. Soon, an aperitif with the retirees, then an early dinner, and a new round of gaffes by the Dalton brother. I can think of worse ways to spend an evening.

The train stops at Kalgoorlie, Western Australia. There's time for a little sightseeing. The taxi driver points out the apocalyptic Super Pit, an open-cut gold mine, brightly lit up. The trucks, down at the bottom of the mine, look like toys. Then he decides that since I'm Italian, I need to get to know the traditions that my compatriots brought so successfully to the antipodes. We arrive at 133 Hay Street. The neon sign reads, in Italian: QUESTA CASA. Literally, "This House." Underneath, in English, THE ONLY HISTORICAL BROTHEL IN AUSTRALIA. I explain to the young woman at the door that I'm a writer, and that I'm interested in finding out more about the history of this brothel. She looks at me, she smiles, and she doesn't believe me.

Interesting place, Kalgoorlie. A city of mines, brisk, no-nonsense people, straight streets, and bars where young women in panties and bras—skimpies, as they're called here—serve beer to strong men wearing the jumpsuits they work in. In my pocket I have a small book I've brought with me from Italy: *Diario australiano*, written by Rodolfo Sonego (1921–2000), the screenwriter, who worked regularly with Alberto Sordi, one of the most popular Italian actors of the twentieth century. They are the notes, newly published, of the location scouting he did for the movie *Bello, onesto, emigrato Australia sposerebbe compaesana illibata (A Girl in Australia)*, which came out in 1971. It's the story of a poor emigrant who marries a beautiful compatriot by correspondence; it is not, however, until she lands in Australia that he discovers she is a prostitute; he accepts her anyway.

I learn from my reading that Rodolfo Sonego, charmed by the location, got off his train here, in Kalgoorlie of all places. The Railway Hotel still stands on the square across from the railway station, but you can no longer find Frank, the Sardinian immigrant, who told Sonego, "Yes, it's all gold here: right behind the courtyard there's a gold mine." Also long gone is Mr. Recchia, who woke up every day at noon; Pietro, the miner from Bergamo, according to whom "taking an Australian girl to bed is like drinking a barrel of beer." No more immigrants gambling away the gold they've found playing Two-Up (a heads or tails coin-toss game, with a twist); instead of gambling it away, they might give their gold to a young Sicilian girl because "they wanted to make love in Italian." Still, something remains in the air from those days: don't ask me why.

Tuesday, Fourth Day

My third night on the Indian Pacific would have been peaceful if it hadn't been for my cell phone, which suddenly got reception and started working again. It was a call from the producer of an Italian television program; she didn't believe I was *really* on a train in the Australian desert, and she wouldn't let me go.

Bright blue spring morning, big sky. It's my son's birthday on the other side of the world. I get out at Perth, Western Australia, on the Indian Ocean. I find that this city has only two shortcomings: not enough taxis and a few too many flies. Otherwise, the air is clear: everything lit up brightly. John Kinder, a professor of Italian Studies at the University of Western Australia, tells me: "Perth is a frontier city, and people take initiatives. If you don't do things for yourself, no one will do them for you." Perth—the name is Scottish—is the most isolated metropolis on earth. The closest big city is on Bali, in Indonesia.

The combination of glass and green spaces, river and ocean; the neatly tended neighborhoods; a general air of prosperity, in part due to a thriving mining industry, with eager Chinese customers—the place is humming so efficiently you start to feel vaguely suspicious: can it all be true? The many Italian expatriates I talk to all confirm. A few of them suggest an explanation: the immigration policies. Realistic or pitiless: take your choice. It's no longer a "White Australia" policy, the way it used to be: what counts now isn't your skin color, but your level of education, your skills, your age, your state of health, and what you can contribute to society. A student can stay for several months on a working holiday visa; for adults, the rules are far tougher. The program includes three streams of immigrants: qualified immigrants (skilled stream); family unification (family stream); political refugees and victims of persecution (humanitarian stream). Applicants are selected through use of a point system: they must be younger than forty-five (unless they're bringing a business with them) and they must meet certain legal and medical standards. (The same is true in New Zealand; I know a successful Italian professional who was required to trim down from 300 pounds to 230 before he could be issued a visa.) In other words, Australia has a plan, pursued for years, even at the cost of considerable hardships, by conservative and liberal administrations alike.

////////////////////

We Italians arrived in Australia in waves, and each wave left its mark: at the turn of the twentieth century, from northern Italy, to work in the mines; under Fascism, only to find ourselves labeled enemy aliens during the war and being interned. After the restoration of diplomatic relations (1948), Italians poured into Australia, especially from southern Italy, after a monthlong voyage by ship. Italian immigrants were second in number only to those from Great Britain: 360,000 people from 1947 to 1974. Italian immigrants would take any work that was available: they were miners in the west, sugarcane harvesters in the northeast, bricklayers and blue-collar workers everywhere. Some of the immigrants made their fortunes. In a restaurant here in Perth, I was introduced to Tom D'Orsogna, born in 1918, who produces cold cuts and salami, and who dresses just like Robert Redford in *The Great Gatsby*. In Canberra, I spoke to Signor Pastrello, originally from Brescia, who now manages racehorses and soccer players, but certainly remembers where he started: "We weren't afraid of snakes, in the plantations of Queensland. We were so pissed off that as soon as the snakes saw us, they turned tail to get away."

I see lots of young Australians of Italian heritage here in Perth. I've seen plenty more in Sydney, Melbourne, and Adelaide as well. The impression I get is that they live in a sort of limbo: sort of Italian in

Australia, decidedly very Australian when they go back to Italy on vacation or to visit family. In contrast with their parents—who tended to marry other sons and daughters of Italian immigrants—they find husbands and wives anywhere in Australian society. Australia's multicultural immigration policy helped a great deal, and nowadays Italian Australians constitute a model minority. A minority, nonetheless, with some issues of identity. This is no longer the old Australia that looked askance at Italians born anywhere south of Livorno, but the national identity remains white, Anglo-Saxon, and Protestant. You can find excellent soccer and cappuccino here, by now, but rugby and beer carry greater weight.

While their Italian parents and grandparents worry about their pensions, the new Italian Australians seem well-disposed toward Italy, and vice versa. Loretta Baldassar, an anthropologist at the University of Western Australia and the author of a history of Veneto migrants to Australia (*From Paesani to Global Italians*, 2005), tells me about it (in English): "The prejudices associated with the first immigrants (dark, dirty, unreliable) have been replaced by positive connotations. These days, Italy is viewed as a cultivated nation, sophisticated, well dressed, well nourished. Today there's a considerable symbolic social capital in being Italian." This view is confirmed by Maria Di Giambattista, who appears at a public conference in a black dress, with her hair up in a bun: "At school, fifty years ago, my classmates made fun of me because I ate bread that wasn't square and that dripped olive oil. Now, in any good restaurant, that's exactly what they're ordering."

Northbridge, Perth's old Italian neighborhood, is now full of Asian bars and parking structures, and membership in the WA Italian Club on Fitzgerald Street, founded in 1934, has declined from seven thousand to thirteen hundred. The tenor Beppe Bertinazzo and his recollections of La Scala aren't enough to draw in the children of the children of the Italians. The club has to employ skimpies, or scantily clad barmaids, for Friday night shifts. Those skimpies are serving tonight, as well, and they shake their hips fetchingly as they move from table to table. Signora Christine Madaschi, a member of the club's board, disapproves but is willing to tolerate.

All the same, Italy—blurred, magical, idealized—is still there, like an island on the horizon. Everyone at the club was highly amused that I had arrived from Sydney by train. Surrounded by billiards tables and faded photographs, they talk about soccer. In English, true, but still, soccer is what they're talking about. During the World Cup, they almost all rooted for Italy. The only time their conscience bothered them was when the Italian Azzurri played the Australian Socceroos. Then someone in the crowd pointed out that, after all, having *two* teams you feel passionate about was an ideal situation: "We can't lose!"

You can't get any more Italian than that.

5

From the Atlantic to the Pacific: Last Train for Obama

Grab your ticket and your suitcase
Thunder's rolling down this track

BRUCE SPRINGSTEEN, "LAND OF HOPE AND DREAMS"

Go West, (Not So) Young Man!

On the Amtrak train no. 693, the Downeaster, for Portland, Maine, the horn blows incessantly. It blows when it leaves Boston's North Station; it blows when it enters the rain-swept little stations of New Hampshire; it blows as it passes the white houses, emblems of New England. It blows as it passes through forests of pine and silver birch, for no apparent reason: maybe the train thinks it's a ship, and it sees harbors everywhere. I'm told that this is what American trains have to do, because the level crossings are unguarded. I'm not entirely convinced. Someone's having too much fun with these Atlantic horns.

I like Amtrak's trains: they're not fast, but they get there. Shiny as bullets, low and narrow, comfortable but not too comfortable, they display the practical cleanliness of motels, where a stain isn't considered an unforgivable sin. These are the trains of a Spartan nation, which we are preparing to cross.

Today we're just working our way up to the starting line: doing a test lap, like a Grand Prix race driver. We're going from Boston,

Massachusetts, to Portland, Maine—the state of lobsters, Stephen King, and Liv Tyler, an outlying eastern province, solitary and slightly anarchic. Tomorrow, we head west. Our destination: the other ocean. We're going to cross fifteen states and—if God and the railroads are willing—we'll arrive in Portland, Oregon. From the Atlantic to the Pacific, we'll try to understand what's stirring in the belly of America during the run-up to the 2012 presidential election.

While the train sounds its horn—ignored by human beings and pets alike—I consider the fact that it's been thirty-five years since my first trip to the United States. Summer 1977, I was twenty years old. That time, too, coast-to-coast (and back!), with five friends and a motor home rented in Pennsylvania, and reserved by means of long, anxious, staticky intercontinental phone calls. Maps from the American Automobile Association (AAA) in hand, Fleetwood Mac on the car radio, and one phone call a week to our parents, collect. This time, arriving by plane, I photographed and tweeted out the shape of the clouds over the North Atlantic (Lufthansa hot spot).

But the yearning remains the same. The same conviction that America is an endlessly renewable mystery that bears studying: it changes continuously, and its strength lies in the way it keeps changing. This time, we'll try to do it from a European point of view. A pair of German eyes—belonging to Karl Hoffmann—and a number of Italian eyes: mine and those of Andrea Salvadore (director), Alberto Engeli and Gianni Scimone (cameramen), and Soledad Ugolinelli (producer). In fact, during this trip we'll produce a daily video blog and a TV program.

We're off to discover America, then. Columbus is taking the train this time. "Go west, young man!" suggested Horace Greeley, born in these parts (Amherst, New Hampshire), in 1811. I'm no longer a young man, but you know what? Tomorrow, I'm going west all the same.

Portland, Maine–Boston, Massachusetts

Portland, Maine. It's pouring down rain. We have an appointment to meet in a diner called the Miss Portland at seven in the morning. When I ask for further details about the early meeting, they tell me that that's when Americans eat breakfast—as if that explained anything. Rachel, in a candy pink uniform, offers us luxurious cakes—actual chocolate cakes, tall as row houses in the West Village—and tirelessly offers refills on our huge *caffè lungo*, as Italians call American coffee, a consolation of American dawns and a conquest of Western civilization. The diner, built in 1949, is modeled on a railroad car. The compartments are gauged to the size of human beings in that period: skinny, apparently. Nowadays a table for four will accommodate two people, or three Europeans.

In any case, they're right. If you're going to start an American journey, you need an American breakfast, and for an American breakfast, you need a German appetite. My traveling companion Karl digs into butter-fried eggs yellow as chicks in the sunshine, charred bacon, toast drowning in butter. Rachel explains that many refugees from the Horn of Africa arrived here in Maine—ninety-seven percent white—because the state has adopted generous social welfare policies.

We talk about it in the taxi on our way to the station. Our driver, Hussein, comes from Djibouti, and he doesn't know that we're talking about him. Even if he did, he wouldn't care: he's too busy fighting his way around puddles and warding off melancholy. The sky is a sheet of cellophane tipped to one side, and it spills water onto Portland, a small city by the sea, a city we're not going to visit. Only surrealistic pictures of lobsters on the darkened neon signs on the restaurants, in the intervals between windshield wipers.

The train for Boston pulls out at eight on the dot. Our long journey to the Pacific, coach class, begins. We board without ceremony. The Downeaster isn't a train for tourists, not on a day like this one. There's a slow leak above seat 16D. The Wi-Fi is working, which comes as a pleasant surprise. Two and a half hours along the Atlantic coastline: nothing much, considering the distances in this country.

The Downeaster for Boston gradually fills up with railway humanity that looks the same everywhere you go: wheeled suitcases, loose comfortable clothing, brief smiles, something to read. Sitting next to me is an oversized young man in Bermuda shorts and flip-flops who's playing on a smartphone and emitting small satisfied grunts. Whenever anyone asks us where we're going, all weighed down with video cameras, computers, and notebooks, we try to tell them that we left this Portland, and we're going to the other Portland. "That's wonderful!" they all reply. But their eyes tell another story: "Why the hell would you go by train? Wouldn't it be faster if you fly?"

Boston, Massachusetts

From the Atlantic to the Pacific, agreed. But next time, maybe let's go from Miami to San Diego. It keeps raining down on this America, and only the bravest young women venture out into the fall-like damp, displaying acres of thighs and optimistic flip-flops. Then we see them slip into the Starbucks on Boylston Street, where they order a bucketful of boiling hot cappuccino.

The chilly city is almost unrecognizable from my previous visits. The distillation of a country that still hasn't warmed up for the coming presidential election. The super PACs, freed of the rules on party financing, raise money that's useful to their own candidate and information that's harmful to his adversary. There's no interview or statement from any of the candidates that hasn't been recorded and dissected, in search of something compromising.

We walk around asking for opinions on the presidential election, but they are not forthcoming. It's not that the Bostonians we meet are wary of inquisitive foreigners; they just seem bored by the subject. "We really need someone to take charge . . . ," yawns a well-dressed woman in her forties, rushing out of a building. "So much can happen between now and November. . . . A week is a long time in politics!" says a young man obviously not scared by platitudes.

The election campaign is going to warm up, just like the spring, but for now things seem quiet, even the malicious delight of the Republicans; seeing the economy struggling and the president in difficulty, they are tempted to put the blame on Europe. At ten in the morning we show up at Mitt Romney headquarters; the candidate is at home here (he was the seventieth governor of Massachusetts). The address is 585 Commercial Street, just a stone's throw from the Garden, where the Boston Celtics play. It's a vaguely unsettling building, without a sign or any distinctive insignia. It's the way I picture the tax office in Paramus, New Jersey.

I know two interesting Italians in Boston. The first is Pier Paolo Pandolfi. They say that he's one of three Italians most likely to get the Nobel Prize for medicine, and he doesn't contradict me when I mention it. I like that about him. Repressed academic ambitions can be harmful, and often in the Italian university system, they have less to do with Nobel Prizes, and more to do with how to land a position for your assistant. PPP—I call him for simplicity's sake—has an impressive CV. He runs genetic cancer research at Beth Israel Deaconess Medical Center, one of the great teaching hospitals at Harvard Medical School. He identified the molecular mechanisms and genetic conditions governing the onset of certain kinds of tumors, and he's trying to find a cure by using murine models (mice). Is he hopeful? "It's now or never," he says concisely. He explains science through a continuous sequence of soccer metaphors. ("Recruiting the best international talents for every position is possible for a major soccer team or a major American university. In Italy, unfortunately, it's not.") I used to think that scientist and AC Milan fan were mutually exclusive: I was misinformed.

Pippo Crotti is thirty-three years old and he practices a different profession. He comes from Romanengo, a few miles outside Crema: a compatriot of mine. The son of the town veterinarian, he was very young when he first went to Los Angeles to study at the Actors Studio. Cirque du Soleil discovered him in a video and hired him, out of a hundred applicants. Pippo invented a character—Valentino, the exaggerated Italian—and now he tours the world with a wife from Pescara (Michela), a young son (Nicolò), and nine suitcases. For the past few weeks they've been here in Boston. Before that, San Diego, San Francisco, Toronto, Montreal, London, Amsterdam, and Baltimore; they're continuing on to Washington, DC, Atlanta, Miami, New York, Philadelphia, Ottawa, and Los Angeles; then Australia, South Korea, Japan, and China.

I ask him, What could Obama and Romney do in the Cirque du Soleil? Contortionist and trapeze artist, he replies. A political scientist couldn't have summed it up any more concisely.

Boston, Massachusetts—Albany, New York

Train no. 499, the Lake Shore Limited for Albany, capital of New York State, is departing Boston's South Station at 11:55 a.m. It's a short train—one locomotive, four cars—where no one phones and almost no one talks. The conductor apologizes: there's no Wi-Fi! Actually, there is (usually it's the other way around). The bar car—white Formica tabletops and banquettes in dark blue Naugahyde—seems like a self-propelled diner: I almost expect to see Rachel, the Portland diner's waitress, come bustling up, with her cakes and her smiles.

We stop in Springfield at 2:17 p.m., but we don't see any of the Simpsons. On the other hand, Gianni Lovato, Milanese, seventy years old, boards the train in Pittsfield. He knew that we'd be coming through. He introduces himself with a bottle of Campari, glasses, and orange peels, potato chips, and homemade hummus. He tells a fascinating story. He came here to upstate New York, in the seventies, attracted by the myth of Woodstock and the new America (also by the female flower children, he confesses). "Ah, what a wonderful time we had! But I didn't dress like the others, you know. I was a plainclothes hippie," he recalls seriously. And then, with a smile: "Let's just say that I was an anarchist nights."

He never left America. For that matter, he won't leave the restaurant car either, even though the Amtrak conductor, stiff and formal, keeps telling him: "I'm very sorry, but it's forbidden to consume food and beverages brought from outside the train!" Gianni Lovato glances at him. "But we're Italians!" he blurts out in English, inviting him to drink a toast. And, surprisingly, the man accepts both the explanation and the glass.

Now Mr. Lovato has a white cat and a Twitter account. As the train passes through the station near his house, a small group of people wave a little Italian flag and a German one, too—all organized by Gianni Lovato, former plainclothes hippie.

The Lake Shore Limited climbs past hills, forests, and rivers. A half-open window at the back of the last car allows you to watch America as it goes streaming past, getting farther and farther from the Atlantic. On board, the USA in miniature: all colors, every age, a diverse array of occupations. Factory workers and college students, silent matrons, teenagers with lots of zits and gadgets, couples embracing and watching a movie on their laptop. One young woman shows off a pair of tattooed feet and a hat with opossum ears. When I ask her why, she looks at me, startled: "Why not?"

When the British playwright Noël Coward was touring the United States in the thirties, he had the names of the actors written on the sides of the railway cars, and the names lit up when the train passed through the stations, so that the waiting travelers could applaud. Personally, I'm satisfied with the show I'm seeing: America streaming past, rocked from side to side.

In Albany—which to me looks like a miniature Washington, DC—we have an appointment at the New York State Assembly with Ron Canestrari, the majority leader. He's an affable man, a professional politician, with an Italian look and an American attitude. We talk about the forthcoming election—he's a Democrat—then he escorts me into the main hall, where the Assembly is currently in session. As soon as I walk in, the chairman welcomes me, reads out my biography, and asks for a round of applause. I'm still baffled when Assemblyman Matthew Titone approaches and says hello. "I'm openly Italian and openly gay," he announces. When I ask him which is more demanding, he pauses. "Being openly Italian has its challenges. But it's more difficult to be openly gay," he concludes. Then he pinches my cheeks, smiles to the video camera, and leaves.

Toward Cleveland, Ohio

For the trip from Albany, New York, to Cleveland, Ohio, Amtrak has assigned us a sleeperette. Always beware of diminutives, in whatever language. Especially in the sectors of real estate and transportation.

What is a sleeperette (or roomette, according to another school of thought)? A cubicle where you can have a good time provided you're a Pilates instructor. All other human beings—including us—can only look on, with mystical stupor. The only place set aside for luggage is a space over the door—ideal for stowaways, lovers, and any corpses you might need to hide, but not great for a heavy suitcase. The upper bunk runs on a curved, vertical rail. The first step pulls out and transforms into a toilet; the second becomes a sink. I don't want to think what will happen tonight if someone climbs down from the upper bunk when his traveling companion forgot to lower the lid.

Full of railway amazement, we troop off to dinner. We share a table with an agreeable veteran of the Vietnam War, who never actually made it to Vietnam. The U.S. Navy, he tells us, sent him to New Zealand instead, and he, perhaps in gratitude, has just marched fifty years

later in the parade of the Vietnam Veterans of America. From Boston
he's returning home to Milwaukee, Wisconsin. As the daylight fades,
he explains that we're running along next to the Erie Canal, the water-
way that extends from Albany to Buffalo, thus connecting the Hudson
River, and therefore the Atlantic, and the Great Lakes.

Poetry and geography recede into the background, however, out-
shone by a waiter who seems to have jumped out of a musical comedy
and an esoteric menu: some dishes are on the menu but not available;
others are available but not on the menu. . . . No one complains. Trains
in America are a world all their own, populated by young people, old
people, eccentrics, misanthropes, philanthropists, artists, and poor
people (or some combination thereof). On our way back to our overnight accommodations, we run into a young man playing the trumpet,
sitting between two cars, indifferent to the jolting and screeching. He's
heading for Chicago, where he's a music teacher. "I take Amtrak and
not the plane because it's so noisy: I can practice and I don't bother
anyone," he says, as if it were the most logical thing in the world. "I like
the vibe of the train."

I shut the door to my sleeperette, I clamber up to the second story,
I read Don DeLillo's *Americana* on my iPad, and I find it consoling: it's
nice to know that we're not the only lunatics with an unrestrainable
desire to cross the USA. I fall asleep around midnight, in a position
befitting a fakir. At 3:40 a.m. I'm awakened by two sharp raps on the
door. I shut my bag, drag the suitcase, get out of the train, and join the
others on the platform in the Cleveland station.

The night is warm; the sky is clear; the white letters spelling out
CLEVELAND BROWNS STADIUM glitter behind the chain-link fence. Three
skyscrapers rear up over the silver train as it leaves without us, on its
way to Chicago.

Everything looks peaceful and perfect, somehow. But we cannot
afford to stay romantic for too long. We need to find a taxi, pronto. At
four in the morning, no one walks the streets of downtown Cleveland.

Cleveland Rocks!

Cleveland is an interesting city. It doesn't enjoy the best reputation in the rest of the United States. One nickname that's stuck is "the Mistake on the Lake," a moniker that opens itself up to various interpretations: it's either a reference to the city's Municipal Stadium—well-known for being chilly, dreary, and uninviting—or else a sarcastic holdover from the time that the Cuyahoga River actually caught fire, back in 1969, because of the elevated pollution levels at the river's mouth, where it flowed into Lake Erie. It could allude to the city's default on its federal loans in 1978, or be a grim tip of the hat to the spikes in unemployment that plagued Cleveland in the 1980s, when manufacturing in the Midwest, which had long lured immigrants from around the world, first began to collapse.

In any case, things have changed. Cleveland made no further mistakes, and recovery finally came to the city. Heavy manufacturing was replaced by health care, now the city's biggest industry, and to a certain extent that anesthetized the pain, as has been the case elsewhere (in Houston, for instance). Cleveland has been spruced up and now looks clean, full of parks, green spaces, bike paths, and pedestrian malls; in 2005 *The Economist* named Cleveland "one of the most livable cities in America." I have to agree: it's a sort of miniature Chicago, just a little more modest and working-class. "I think I could live here," I tell my traveling companions, who all look at me as if I've lost my mind.

In the warmth of a bright, almost summery sun, we get busy trying to deepen our understanding of the local culture. We discuss politics with those willing to listen (not many), especially in the Tremont neighborhood, full of bright, cheery murals and young people of all colors, long since abandoned by its original immigrants—the Ukrainians, Poles, Hungarians, and Slovaks who came here a century ago to work in the steel mills—now replaced by restaurateurs, baristas, and artists. They seem to be convinced that the Democrats will succeed in taking

Ohio, a fundamental electoral prize: whoever wins Ohio usually wins the election. This is America, I philosophize: always changing, none of that European romanticism about places. They're no better or worse than us, only different.

It's a long day as we wait for the train to Illinois. We search for relics of LeBron James, the basketball champion, born not far away, in Akron, in 1984. We explore the Rock & Roll Hall of Fame, along with crowds of schoolkids on field trips to the museum of America's own classical music: Elvis, Springsteen, Nirvana (in fact, the term "rock 'n' roll" was used here for the very first time, back in 1951, by the DJ Alan Freed). We have lunch with the *Donauschwaben*, the Danube Swabians, Germans who were expelled from Hungary, Romania, and Yugoslavia in the aftermath of the Second World War. They seem to have popped out of a time warp: sandals with socks, vegetables eaten almost raw, stern matrons with sculptural permanents. We even find the time to study up on the real estate market: we discover that 250,000 dollars is all you need to buy a nice house with a big yard overlooking the lake. "Why don't you come back here in winter before making up your minds!" snickers the Realtor who takes us around, skeptical as to our actual intentions to buy.

From Cleveland to Chicago

Some vicious detractors claim that there were other possible trains from Cleveland to Chicago. "It's not true," Soledad, our producer, assures us. "There was only this one, departing at three forty-five a.m. It's not my fault that it's leaving an hour late."

Here we are, under the fluorescent lights of an unlikely early Saturday morning with a map on our knees, a yawn in our throats, and regret in our eyes. We could have slept another hour, before the wake-up call rang us awake with a cheery "Good morning!" "It could have gone worse," Edward says briskly. "It could have snowed." Edward is an Amtrak representative, lives in Florida, and has a robust dislike for snow.

What does it matter? After all, we're here now. We'll wait for the silvery train that runs around the edge of Lake Erie to Toledo, Ohio, and then across Indiana, arriving seven hours later in Chicago, Illinois. Now that I think about it, "run" may not be the exact word I want.

The average speed on long-distance Amtrak trains is seventy-one miles per hour, a joke by European standards. But we don't complain, about the speed of the trains or anything else, and this docile pliability surprises the Americans we meet. The railway, for long trips, is considered an unusual, even eccentric means of transportation. A train isn't patriotic like a car or indispensable like a plane. The idea that someone would choose it to cross America is viewed as strange, almost suspicious.

The sleeperette, upon our second acquaintance, almost seems cozy. I manage to unhook the upper bunk without decapitating myself, for example. And from there, stretched out, I watch the United States go rolling past, like a documentary without voice-over. The cars on the divided roadways move slowly, like in a movie. Boundless fields, farmhouses, brightly lit signs: it all feels like I've seen it before. No one ever goes to America: you can only return.

The state of Ohio gave birth to General Custer, several presidents, LeBron James, George Clooney, and Clark Gable, a wind turbine salesman heading for Illinois informs me. At breakfast I share the table with Don and Dottie—he's seventy-five; she's sixty-five—who are celebrating their forty-first wedding anniversary. They're returning from Niagara Falls to their home in Austin, Texas, by way of Chicago. They say that the reason people are so hostile to Obama is that he's black, just like them. They'll probably vote for him. But they're still going to have to think it over, because they didn't like some of the things that the president said. I take a wild guess: his support for gay rights? Dottie narrows her eyes and bites her lip: I guessed it.

Strange moods are crisscrossing the United States. After thirty-five years spent studying the place, and a few days aboard a train, I know how to recognize the grimaces on the face of a friendly nation. Most

American citizens have moved so often, switched so many jobs, seen so many things change, that they've lost their orientation and their place in America, thinks Salvatore Scibona, a writer from Cleveland and the author of *The End*. A summary that I subscribe to, even though I wish I didn't. Or maybe it's the sleeperette effect: it makes you literary.

Chicago, Illinois

Chicago is the most interesting city in the United States; if you want me to change my mind, you'd have to talk me into spending a winter here. But the wind in the Windy City, in June, is warm and gentle, like the mood of all the people you meet.

We've come to Cellular Field, the ballpark of the White Sox, who are playing Houston today. The sound of bat on ball marks the beginning of nice weather, a potent evocation of summer to which Americans respond with a Pavlovian reflex. Baseball is practically incomprehensible to us foreigners. Still, there is a solution: give up trying to understand it. You don't have to. Baseball is something you inhale, like the warm June air. When a ball is hit out of the park, it has an aesthetic quality and a dynamic immediacy. And if everyone around you is yelling, then you yell, too: there must be a good reason.

Baseball involves a passion for numbers, statistics, rituals, heroes that pop out of nowhere, choreographies, strategies, force, and the control of force. Baseball—162 games a year versus the 16 of football—is the American touchstone, a tireless producer of family memories. The sheer number of children present at Cellular Field proves that all this will continue. It's no accident that so many writers and so many actors have taken on the challenge of this theme: from Don DeLillo's *Underworld* to *Moneyball* with Brad Pitt.

Barack Obama has spent time in this stadium. In the eighties, when he first arrived in Chicago to work as a community organizer, he moved to a house not far from here. We ride bikes over to see the street, the barbershop, the restaurant, and the cafeteria he frequented. In Italy no one would dream of visiting the family home of a former president or prime minister (Silvio Berlusconi's, being so colorful, might be an exception). But in the U.S., there are political pilgrimages, which have nothing to do with your party affiliation. A president is a historic personage; you go to see where he came from in order to understand him. Which is an illusion, but it's fun to foster illusions while pedaling around Hyde Park.

From Chicago to Milwaukee, Wisconsin

We're traveling on Canadian tracks toward Wisconsin, which isn't in Canada. An oddity that can be explained only by the free markets of railroads. Amtrak is the owner of some stretches of track (the most important is the line from Boston to Washington, DC). It rents all the other tracks from their owners. The tracks that are taking us from Chicago to Milwaukee today, for example, are the property of the Canadian National Railway.

We have other disappointments. "Two of you can ride in the locomotive!" they had promised us. I'd immediately volunteered, along with the cameraman Alberto "Peace" Engeli, who owed his new nickname to the fact that, while wandering around the South Side of Chicago (80 murders and 260 gun-related injuries in the last sixteen months), he aimed his video camera at worrisome-looking individuals while shouting "Peace!" The interesting thing is that those guys, instead of coming after us, just returned the greeting.

We return to the train. When the time comes to climb into the engine, we discover that in the cockpit there is room for only one guest; of course I make way for the video camera. A pity. Every man, when he was a teenager, dreamed of driving a train, Freud explained, attributing a sexual significance to this desire. I return to the car a little frustrated (of course! Freud would have said). I sit down and listen to the railway lesson offered by a loquacious Amtrak employee who's traveling with us.

I learn the following about American trains:

1. Passenger traffic has collapsed since the 1950s, as a result of the development of the Interstate Highway System and the growth of commercial aviation. And it's never recovered.

2. The American railroads focus on freight. That's why, on many lines, freight trains take precedence.

3. A freight train is on average 1.2 miles long.

4. Our train is pulled by the engine to Milwaukee; then it will be pushed backward back to Chicago. That's why it's called a "push-pull train."

The lesson doesn't last long, and neither does the trip. At noon I see Milwaukee again for the first time in twenty years, when it was a blue-collar city that was changing its skin. Today it looks cleaned up, with a festive green lakefront. The railway station is white and graceful; the urban renewal is impeccable; there's even a museum designed by the architect Santiago Calatrava, which folds its wings—literally—at five in the afternoon. Our immigrant compatriots have built the Italian Community Center and are preparing for their annual festival. Mario Calini, the only one who speaks Italian, welcomes us. He becomes emotional when we arrive; he becomes emotional when we leave; he worries when we ask those present whether the Italians of Milwaukee are more Democratic or Republican (the latter, if I understood correctly).

In Milwaukee, the whites (chiefly of German and Polish origin) constitute forty percent of the population, and live separately; there are an equal number of blacks and they live to the north of the city; the Hispanics (seventeen percent) live in the south; the Asians, especially those of the Hmong ethnic group, live to the northwest. Milwaukee is a simple city and a city of symbols: Harley-Davidson motorcycles, Miller beer, the TV series *Happy Days* (there's even a statue of Fonzie, bronze jacket and both thumbs up). A no-frills America, and I'm not going to add any of my own.

From Wisconsin to North Dakota

We're practically halfway there. After leaving Milwaukee, we're on our way to Fargo and Rugby, North Dakota: the geographic center of the North American continent. From *Happy Days* to the Coen brothers' *Fargo*: a culturally and climatically interesting transition.

I'm happy I chose to cross the USA by train—if for no reason other than to see the faces of Americans when I tell them: astonishment, consternation, admiration, and compassion, all in a single glance. "Why?" After ten days of travel, more than two thousand miles of rails, and many baffled faces, I've drawn up a reply. Actually, fifteen of them, one for each hour of travel that awaits us today.

1. Because last year we took the train from Moscow to Lisbon, and at that point, there was no more land to cross. So we just started over again on this side.

2. Because a train is a rolling theater, where the scenery and actors change constantly.

3. Because a train is a plot all ready and waiting. Comedy and tragedy; though the first is better, all things considered.

4. Because outside the windows, there's America on parade, and it's impossible to tear your eyes away.

5. Because every once in a while, it's nice to be a stranger in a strange land.

6. Because on a long journey, your thoughts get longer, and they take on a surprising clarity.

7. Because Amtrak is a stars-and-stripes lesson in stoicism.

8. Because the air is clear, the colors are bright, and the spaces are immense (the sleeping compartments, on the other hand, are small, agreed).

9. Because repacking your suitcase every day is a Zen exercise.

10. Because it's nice to be lazy while on the move.

11. Because you can talk, when you get tired of reading. And watch, when you're tired of talking.

12. Because everywhere, we find Italians who help us, encourage us, guide us, and correct us.

13. Because today we're traveling on a train that's called the Empire Builder and we're interviewing people with names like Rocky (commissioner, City of Milwaukee).

14. Because North Dakota is one of the few states that, in my many trips to America, I still haven't visited. And I liked the ads for Montana canned meat when I was a boy ("Down in Montana where the cowboys herd cattle / the struggle for justice is a genuine battle").

15. Because the idea of giving up travel is irrelevant at age twenty, at thirty it's pleasant, and at forty it's understandable. But at fifty it's just plain reckless.

Rugby, North Dakota: The Center of America

In the last twenty-four hours we've met a park ranger with a plush catfish in his bag; a couple from Savannah, Georgia, who are traveling by train at their doctor's orders; a deputy sheriff who was kind enough to let us ride in his squad car; an ex-mayor who's become an undertaker with a 1968 Cadillac convertible; the editor in chief of the daily newspaper the *Tribune*, who sells stationery in her newsroom; the owner of radio KZZJ AM 1450, whose sons are in the National Guard; and a young female soccer player named Bailey, immediately nicknamed Miss North Dakota.

Miss North Dakota! We like the sound of it. Bailey moved here from California and works with her family at the Cornerstone Cafe. Just outside the restaurant, a rock obelisk announces: GEOGRAPHICAL CENTER OF NORTH AMERICA. Fascinating: as long as you don't come to Rugby ready to pick nits. There are others who claim that the exact location is in a marsh two miles outside downtown Rugby. Others say that the center of the North American continent is located farther east, near Devils Lake. Fourth version: the obelisk was erected in 1931 by the local Lions Club near a restaurant, which was moved in 1971. The proprietors took it with them, and they installed it in front of their new location. Geography at the service of commerce: viva l'America!

North Dakota! The state with the lowest rate of unemployment in the USA. The oil boom is attracting people from all over the Union. A controversial extraction technique (hydraulic fracturing or fracking) produces half a million barrels of crude oil a day, and could give the U.S. energy self-sufficiency by 2030. Home prices have doubled, and it's impossible to find workers in the drilling area; the McDonald's in Williston reaches out two hundred miles away to find employees. New people are constantly arriving in North Dakota, and the economy is thriving. "Here in Rugby even the prison is thriving, after folding years ago for lack of prisoners," Dale G. Niewoehner, owner of the Cadillac, three churches, the funeral parlor, and a patriotic stars-and-stripes tie, tells us with some satisfaction.

Rugby, North Dakota! One radio station, one motel, no taxis. A patrol car meets us at the train station and gives us a lift to the motel. They love to have visitors up here, the policeman at the wheel explains.

The population is 2,879; the last murder, he informs us, dates back to 1963. I'm pretty sure we won't modify those figures: we won't settle in Rugby and we won't have children here, nor shoot anyone.

We walk everywhere with our noses in the air, like the greenest of tourists. The sky seems three-dimensional; the clouds have muscles. In the winter, they assure us, it's very cold. It's no accident that the people who settled here in the late nineteenth century came from Germany and Norway: they felt right at home. Still today, the two ethnic groups constitute seventy-eight percent of the population. My traveling companion, Karl Hoffmann, has learned that a Mrs. Hoffmann lives here, and he's made arrangements to meet her. But the lady doesn't show up, and he grumbles about the general unreliability of Germans.

We like North Dakota. It's the illegitimate offspring of the railroad (Great Northern Railway, 1890–1970), and the name of the train that brought us here today—and will take us away again tomorrow—commemorates the fact: Empire Builder. A protein-driven, pragmatic, optimistic America, not particularly given to subtleties.

The Empire of Fracking

They shouldn't call it the Empire Builder. They should change the name to Delay Builder, considering how much it accumulates. We arrived in Rugby, North Dakota, two hours late. We were supposed to leave Rugby at 7:07 a.m. for Malta, Montana: the train finally got moving at 9:33. In no particular hurry. They even moved it a hundred yards to help us load our luggage.

Yesterday we spent the day with Dale G. Niewoehner, the former mayor, who works out of his house: on the ground floor, a funeral home (with coffins on display, cremation urns, and a laboratory for the preparation of the corpse); upstairs, a living room, a bedroom, and relics of cruise liners (including the *Andrea Doria*), a collection of bricks from famous buildings, and a buffalo head. Today, with his wife, Marilyn ("We met at a funeral"), he took us to the station and explained why Amtrak, on this stretch of the line, is often (always?) late. The tracks belong to the Burlington Northern Santa Fe (BNSF) railway, which always gives precedence to freight trains. Passengers can wait.

The Empire Builder will cross North Dakota, Montana, and a corner of Idaho as it heads for Seattle, Washington. Aboard the train we meet Mandy, who's going from Minnesota to see a friend in Williston, Montana, at the heart of the new oil boom. "It's a crazy place," she explains. "At McDonald's and Walmart they pay twenty bucks an hour, three times as much as in New York, and they still can't hold on to their employees. Working on the wells, the guys get thirty bucks an hour at the very least. They're coming here from all over America. Lots of men, lots of alcohol. I've seen guys fighting over a girl. Testosterone and petroleum. Wow!"

Mandy's friend works for twenty-five dollars an hour, cleaning up oil spills, things like that. Fracking calls for the pumping of liquids or gases under high pressure deep underground in order to break up layers of rock, and there is a risk of damaging the water table. In some places, it is said, drinking water has become flammable. Before we stop, I suggest to Soledad, our producer, an experiment for the video cameras: she can get out at Williston, drink from the faucet, and then light a cigarette. But she's not about to fall for it; she's from Rome. "I don't smoke," she replies.

Just before we cross the Montana border, a new time zone. In Montana the sky is gray and light blue; big bellying clouds get a running start across the plains. Every so often it rains briefly. The oil wells stop; the light-colored low hills begin. The semitrailers leave dust trails.

In midafternoon, three hours late, we arrive in Malta, Montana. The name was chosen by a Great Northern executive who decided to spin the globe: his finger landed on the island in the Mediterranean. Sunshine, wind, eight streets, the Lucky Bullet bar, and a few pickup

trucks with rifles in the gun rack. The owner of the Maltana Motel—
the only motel in town—seems surprised by our arrival. But then, so
are we, come to think of it.

Martians in Montana

While you're waiting to fall asleep, it's nice to hear the sound of trains,
wrote Don DeLillo. Maybe he'd taken a room at the Maltana Motel in
Malta, Montana, and he wasn't troubled by insomnia. The massive
freight trains of the BNSF continue to pass by, and let's just say that
they don't pass unobserved. They plunge wailing over the unmanned
level crossing and then vanish over the distant plains. Two Herculean
locomotives, two hundred stack cars loaded with containers, many of
them with Chinese writing on the side. From west to east, from east to
west, tireless nocturnal roars.

At eight thirty p.m., still in bright daylight (it's now mountain time),
we were already shut up in our respective motel rooms. An hour later,
my companions, I'll learn the following morning, knocked on my door
to inform me that an appointment was canceled. Come on, guys. If two
hundred railcars can't wake me up, how on earth are the knuckles of a
well-mannered young Italian woman going to do it?

Malta is a place Wim Wenders would have loved: a film set waiting
for a film. Straight roads, right angles, cobalt sky, and faded signs. The
local attractions are the remains of a dinosaur (Leonardo) and the out-
law Kid Curry (Harvey Logan), who robbed a train a few miles from
here in 1901. That was the last robbery the Wild Bunch pulled, before
Butch Cassidy and the Sundance Kid fled to South America.

We wander through empty streets, cut horizontally by beams of
sunlight, until they invite us to come on in at the Lucky Bullet bar:
courteously, without drawing a gun on us. The American West we
know from movies, the minute we draw a little closer, breaks down into
real-life stories, personal and often tough. Jane, at the bar, shows us a

photograph of her daughter's father, who left the day before for Afghanistan; her girlfriends tell us of a small town that's supportive but nosy; Dennis and Dodee show off the saddle they won at the rodeo.

Next door, an auction of bric-a-brac attracts a little crowd. On the shelves is the everyday history of America. Tiny objects, small home appliances, cheap memorabilia that someone treasured, are now all lined up to gather dust and casual glances. Not far away, at the restaurant in the Great Northern Hotel—a piece of railway time travel—the twenty-three-year-old Krystal, a good-looking blonde with messy hair, shows off her gleaming, enameled fingernails to the video camera; at last something happens around here, her eyes clearly state. She explains that she came here from Portland, Oregon, in search of work. She found it immediately, but she doesn't know how long she'll stay.

At seven in the morning—brilliant sunshine, as if someone had polished the sky the night before—we meet an engineer with three young daughters. They took two rooms at the Maltana Motel. Their car is parked outside their door like a horse next to a campsite. The girls are eating breakfast on the hood of the car, in preparation for a swim meet. I'd love to chat about the forthcoming presidential election, but it would be cruel at this hour, and I don't.

We spend the rest of the day wandering along the tracks, while waiting to reboard the Empire Builder and head west. Right now, the train is two hours late, but that could become three hours, or just one: Amtrak is a form of life lesson. Big sky / some rain / no train: that's fine, though. After all, we kind of asked for it. We came by train, and we have no car, which in these latitudes is inconceivable.

Four Italians, a Swiss, and a German visiting the one museum in town, talking about dinosaurs, and kicking at garbage along the track bed.

Martians in Montana.

The Green Cushion of the Pool Table

A man who claimed he had been hit by a bullet fired from a speeding car while he was in Montana working on a book, to be called *Kindness in America*, has confessed that he actually shot himself. The sheriff's office believes that this was a desperate act of self-promotion, but provided no further details.

How can a place like this help but capture the imagination? The item is front-page news in the daily paper, the *Great Falls Tribune*, and it casts a garish pop light on Montana. As we arrive by train from the Great Plains, the spectacle is magnificent: the Rocky Mountains close off the horizon to the west, like the cushion of an immense pool table. Then the train runs along the river and climbs up toward Glacier National Park. The greenery glistens with rain; there are lots of hoodies and fleeces. We arrive at Lake McDonald—it's the actual name; there are no sponsorship deals involved—but we can go no farther: the pass is snowed in. It's June, I'll remind you.

In the national parks, either it's raining or it's just stopped raining, or else it's about to rain; that's one thing I've learned in thirty-five years of traveling in America. It's enough to take a quick look around and you can understand why this country produces so much fine film and television. There are the backgrounds, there are the characters, and they both speak eloquently.

Americans, especially outside the big cities, are well-disposed toward foreigners. We've met and talked to hundreds of people, from the Atlantic to here. No one has ever refused to answer our questions.

Glacier National Park is no exception. In the wet park, with blue-green lakes and ice in the distance, we meet Montana families with young daughters eager to travel to Africa; a couple of gray-haired ladies unsure whether to pursue the allure of a grizzly bear or that of a gin and tonic; a young conservative from Spokane, proud of his blue-collar city; two brothers who operate a mountain hut for hikers, furious with

American politics in general and angry at Washington, DC, in particular. "They lie to us!" they shout, taking turns.

"What about?" I ask, politely.

"Everything!" they shout back

At the Polebridge entry station we meet a park ranger with a ponytail under the regulation ranger hat. He's originally from the Black Forest (Germany) and he knows all about Milan, where he lived for three years, working as an engraver. Karl, euphoric at the unexpected appearance of a compatriot, asks in English: "Have you seen any bears around here?" But he gets the pronunciation wrong: instead of *bear*, he says *beer*. The Teutonic ranger maintains his composure: "A beer? I'd love one. But I can't drink on duty." Then he laughs: "No bears today."

If David Lynch had spent the day with us, he could have done the entire casting for a new season of *Twin Peaks*. I would gladly have taken a walk-on part. A fisherman, maybe. The kind who watches the world go by, and smiles.

Spokane and the Future

Anybody who comes to Spokane and exclaims: "What a lovely city!" should probably be given a Breathalyzer test. But it's not a simple city either. It's hard to get around on foot, it's challenging to visit in June— fifty degrees Fahrenheit and wind that'll whip a newspaper right out of your hands—and it's difficult to pronounce. It's *Spō-kan*, with the emphasis on *kan*. It was the name of a native tribe, and it means "children of the sun." I have to say, I haven't even seen the sun.

Still, Spokane—in Washington State, near the Idaho line—is an interesting place. A city that is in no way weighed down by the burden of its reputation, in part because few Americans even know where it is. A friendly place, delighted to be the subject of attention. The editor of the *Spokesman-Review* (founded in 1894) threw open the doors to his newsroom, introduced us to his reporters, and invited us out to dinner.

A pragmatic, rapidly changing city, Spokane sometimes gives the impression it doesn't know exactly where it's going, but it keeps going all the same, and that redounds to its honor.

We got here at three in the morning, after departing from Montana. Train stations at night have a particular allure, though it's sometimes hard to capture if you've just spent eight hours aboard an Amtrak train (without sleeping berths and running two hours late, so no surprise there). We head straight for our beds at the Hotel Lusso. The name means "luxury" in Italian, but don't be fooled. It's an absolutely unexceptional place. If there's any luxury around, you'll find it in the hotel around the corner, the majestic Davenport. In 1914, it was the first hotel in America to feature air-conditioning; before giving their guests change, they'd polish the coins until they looked newly minted (an early and innocent forerunner of "money laundering," come to think of it).

A century ago, the money that circulated in Spokane came from the mines, the lumber mills, and the railroads, which also brought many Italians here. A prosperity that endured only a few years, but left lasting traces. Among the regular guests at the Davenport were Bing Crosby, who grew up here, the transatlantic aviator Charles Lindbergh, the actor Bob Hope, and the writer Dashiell Hammett, when he was an operative for the Pinkerton agency. The hotel has recently been restored, and relics of its glory days line the walls. The Davenport has the allure of all hotels that have seen better days: the Adelphi in Liverpool, the Metropol in Moscow, the Plaza in Rome. Places with more mileage behind them than ahead of them.

Like us: the Atlantic is far away, we've almost reached the Pacific, and soon we'll be able to celebrate.

The Ocean in the Background

"Punctually late," says Karl. Amtrak's tactic, so far, seems to be this: never to be on time, but methodically so. In Seattle, on the other hand, we arrived half an hour early. Our American fellow travelers explain skeptically that this is a result of what's known as padding. By this point, there's no doubt that the train will have built up quite a delay; and so on the official schedule, an arrival time is indicated that takes that delay into account. This ploy, more Italian in nature than American, helps to placate the passengers on their arrival. The only ones it made happy was us, because we didn't understand the trick.

In Spokane the Empire Builder is separated into two parts: some cars will go on to Seattle; others will head directly for Portland, Oregon. Even though Portland is our final destination, we've decided to see the Pacific Ocean—it's a matter of principle. We will therefore pass through Everett and Edmonds and arrive in Seattle, the city of Amazon, Nirvana, Boeing, Jimi Hendrix, and Starbucks.

We leave Spokane at 2:20 a.m., after a beer with a view of the waterfall and two hours of provisional sleep. Six zombies try to sleep on the train, but the western dawn doesn't cooperate. The Empire Builder rolls along the Columbia River as the sun peeks under the clouds. Someone announces Icicle Canyon. Frequently people spot elk, beavers, and stags here. Not today. They're probably sleeping. Lucky them.

We roll under the Cascade Range, through the longest railroad tunnel in the U.S. (7.8 miles, completed in 1929), and continue toward Skykomish, amidst forests of pine and Norway spruce.

On this leg of the trip, the sleeping car attendant has a gleam in his eye. His name is Kevin H., or at least that's what his badge assures us. He knows both geography and spelling: if he utters the name of a place, he also explains how to spell it. He's authoritarian, ironic, and scatterbrained: a rare combination, and not just aboard trains. When we ask him permission to do something—can we lower the window while the train is moving at walking speed?—he says "No!" and at the same time nods his head yes. Which means we're all taken care of, both with the rules and with common sense.

Despite my weariness, I've recovered my energy: I give credit to the landscape. Or else, after sixteen days, I've gotten used to the train.

Another forty years and I'll become a professional like the lawyer David Peter Alan, whom we've already met twice during this trip. He spends his life on the rails. "Never taken a plane once in my life!" he proudly declares. Like the pianist in the wonderful film *The Legend of 1900*, who spends his life on an ocean liner, David has transferred his professional and social life onto a means of conveyance. He writes about it and fights to ensure that it's used better. "If one man alone has ridden and described all the rail lines in America, that means there aren't enough of them!" he declares. A little Lincoln of the railways: admirable.

My expertise is marginal at best, in comparison. Let's say that I've acquired certain mechanisms. I know how to pile up my luggage and push it down the train corridors (always use vertical suitcases with four wheels). I know how to open the doors between cars with my foot, and not get hit in the face by them. I know how to drink coffee out of paper cups without burning myself, and how to fold up the tray table without amputating my fingers. I know where the flush button is located in the microbathroom, and I can wash my hands while pushing the faucets with my thumbs. I know exactly where the outlets are located, and I can find them in the dark. I know how to adjust the air, and the location of both the reading light and of the hooks that serve as coatracks and hangers. By now, the sleeperette and yours truly are a battle-tested couple.

The Empire Builder rolls along the Snohomish River valley and we begin to see farmland; pickup trucks, like silent mechanical insects, appear and disappear alongside the train. At 8:50 a.m. we'll arrive at Everett; as he makes the announcement, Kevin H. seems slightly sentimental. When the salt waters of Puget Sound, which opens out into the ocean, appear, we become sentimental ourselves.

We left from the Atlantic; we arrived at the Pacific. We left with the rain, and the rain was awaiting us upon our arrival. In Seattle they say: "We don't tan; we rust." As for us, we don't run that risk. Two days in the city and then we head south, toward the other Portland.

In Amazonia!

The month of June is no guarantee, around here. They call it *Junuary*, a portmanteau of June and January. But we're lucky. The rain at our arrival has given way to blue skies—and let's admit it, we like those better. To the west, beyond Puget Sound, are the Olympic Mountains. To the south is Mount Rainier, with its snowcapped cone. When Seattle decides to pretty herself up, she has few rivals. In the U.S., only Chicago, San Francisco, and New York can compete.

The city center, sloping downhill toward the bay, Pike Place Market, the lakefront in Bellevue, the ups and downs of Madison Avenue, the shops and restaurants of Capitol Hill: everything brightly lit up. The spectacle is so captivating that even Microsoft, a very important resident, appears romantic for a moment (the feeling passes). In order to resist the euphoria, and to celebrate a day without rails, we visit two antithetical places: Amazon and Elliott Bay Book Company. They have books in common, but that's as far as it goes.

At the latter, I meet up with Casey and Rick, whom I first got to know on the publication of my previous books. Both Amazon and Elliott Bay Book Company moved their operations two years earlier, revitalizing—each in its own way—an entire neighborhood. Amazon left the PacMed building, its old redbrick headquarters on Beacon Hill, and moved to South Lake Union. Elliott Bay moved from Pioneer Square, near the bay, to Capitol Hill, on the other side of Interstate 5.

You know about Amazon (because you probably buy things from Amazon): it not only dominates the publishing marketplace; it has invented a new paradigm. You may not know Elliott Bay Book Company, but it was—and remains—the most welcoming bookstore on the West Coast. The bookstore complains that it is considered, by some, to be nothing more than a display window: people come in, they find a book they want, they go home, and they order it from Amazon at a discount. Amazon points out that all industrial revolutions cause disruptions. "After all," the company explains, "we offer our customers a service: it's up to them to decide whether they want it."

I know perfectly well that the matter isn't as simple as that, that it involves issues of competition, copyright, public utility. But on such a beautiful day, let a man who buys lots of books and has written a few have his dreams. Let me say that Amazon is unbeatable when it comes to array of choice and speed of delivery. But a bookstore is unrivaled as a place of social interaction, an opportunity to meet and debate (with booksellers, authors, and other readers). It would be sad to be left alone, with one's book simply delivered to one's door. And it would be absurd to give up the speed, comfort, and convenience of that delivery.

On this day without trains, in the space of a mile and a half, I see a mini Statue of Liberty, a tyrannosaurus under glass, the golden sands of Hawaii, a medieval tower, and two benches side by side: blue for Democrats, red for Republicans.

This is not a psychedelic delirium, and we're not in Florida or Las Vegas, where architectural excess is predictable and encouraged. We're on Lake Washington, the urban lake behind Seattle, home to individuals who have become rich on (our) computers: Bill Gates (Microsoft), Paul Allen (his ex-partner), Jeff Bezos (Amazon), and many others.

The houses run down to the water, the lawns gleam, and today the weather is on our side. You might even see human beings lying on the grass without a windbreaker. In the Medina neighborhood, Bezos's mansion is half-concealed amidst the greenery; Bill Gates's little beach looks soft (*micro*soft?). I don't know who owns the tyrannosaurus, but it's clearly visible inside a glass structure. They tell me that it's set on a platform and that it rears over the indoor pool. Of course it does: who of us hasn't dreamed of swimming under the benevolent gaze of a carnivorous biped that belongs to the saurischian order?

The distance between the pluto-paleontologist of Seattle and the residents of Malta, Montana, is considerable; however, they're still all Americans, and it's possible to find points of contact. For instance, houses, more than clothing or cars, are social indicators, understood and accepted by one and all. The question "Where do you live?" is rarely a matter of innocent curiosity. The answer helps to classify a person. Let us remain in Seattle, or actually Lake Washington: the eastern shore is more desirable than the western one. Over here live the rich, over there the merely well-to-do. Everyone else just goes to the lake on weekends.

Living on a certain street, in the United States, can be a great aid in one's financial and social climbing, and that kind of climbing remains the most widely practiced sport in the country. An American house is a fortress without gates; sometimes, an Italian house is a gate without fortress. The real estate bubble that popped in the USA between 2007 and 2009—triggering financial problems around the world—was caused by the spasmodic desire to buy more house than people could afford.

When I wrote *Ciao, America!: An Italian Discovers the U.S.*, I chose to tell the story of a house, our house in Washington, DC. A house, if you know how to approach it, is the mouth of a tunnel that leads into the American mind. A mind that is no stranger or more complicated than an Italian mind—but it *is* different.

Certainly, it's not easy to understand why a sane man would build a lake house and stick a tyrannosaurus inside it. Wouldn't a triceratops have been enough? It's shorter, and it goes better with the surroundings.

A Polish Blogger Races Toward the Finish Line

The Coast Starlight is almost an elegant train; we're not used to such a thing. From Seattle (King Street Station) it runs south toward Los Angeles and—Amtrak assures us—you can see dolphins from your window. We say so long to Seattle in its customary attire, which we had not yet had a chance to admire: rain and fog, in open defiance of summer.

The train cars date from 1985: aging, but well preserved. There's even a car from 1957, which houses a little movie theater with insanely aggressive air-conditioning (maybe they use it as a freezer for poultry when there's a shortage of passengers). There is a geriatric first class, where the average age is the same as that of the Italian ruling class. We are seated, as usual, in coach. In the seat behind us is Jakub Górski, a Polish blogger who first boarded a train in New York, where he's returning by way of Seattle, Los Angeles, New Orleans, Atlanta, and Washington, DC. Thirteen thousand kilometers (a little over eight thousand miles) in thirteen days, with a super-affordable ticket he bought in London. Jakub doesn't even get a sleeperette: he reclines his seat back and falls asleep under a camo blanket, dreaming of Polish trains. To hear him tell it, they're not much different.

The final day of a long trip is strange, full of bittersweet happiness. Karl, armed with his little video camera, pursues his last few victims; Gianni shoots footage of a young woman's tattoos; Andrea writes; Alberto thinks about Bruce Springsteen and Santa Monica, where he'll return tomorrow. The conductor broadcasts disjointed phrases over the loudspeaker: "In the USA, lollipops are illegal! And it's against the rules to claim your parents are rich if they aren't!" Then he threatens to confiscate all cell phones. Last of all, he reminds us that "smoking aboard trains is a federal offense and those found guilty will be deported to a secret prison in Eastern Europe!" The Polish blogger Jakub listens without turning a hair.

We reach our destination safe and sound. At 1:30 p.m., right on time, we pull into Union Station in Portland, Oregon. We left Portland, Maine, eighteen days ago. Rain here, rain there, sunshine in between. Karl still wants to interview someone. But the passengers are stepping down off the Coast Starlight and slipping away into the rain, becoming memories; and we do the same.

6

From Trieste to Trapani:
Italy in Second Class

I he cafés and restaurants of train stations boast a long
tradition of charm, melancholy, or squalor. . . .
They are particle accelerators,
places of experimentation in emotional physics,
where fission is taken to its logical extreme.

VALERIO MAGRELLI, *LA VICEVITA*

Trieste—Mantua

There are two teenagers at the Trieste train station, the boy dressed as
a cowboy, the girl as a squaw. They are lovely and absurd on this cold,
dark winter morning. They're buying tickets to Venice. It's Fat Tuesday, and Alice and Nicola, thirty-five years of age between them, want
their piece of carnival.

Trieste constitutes an ideal point of departure for my journey across
the country. It is proudly Italian (we fought World War I to get it back
from Austria), but it also feels Slavic (Slovenia is a few miles away). It
looks German (it used to be the main harbor of the Austro-Hungarian
Empire). It is Christian and it is Jewish. It faces the blue Adriatic Sea,
with the green Carso mountains at the back. It's the North of the
South, the South of the North, the East of the West, and the West of
the East.

Great minds met here—Italo Svevo took English lessons from
James Joyce, who made sure he would publish his masterpiece *Zeno's
Conscience* (*La coscienza di Zeno*) in Paris, after local publishers turned it

down. Trieste is brilliant, eccentric, and resilient, and it does nothing the way you'd expect.

I'm starting my journey here, in Italy's northeastern corner, and ending it in Trapani, Sicily—the farthest in Italy you can get from here. From quasi-Germany to near-Africa. The whole way by train, in second-class seats. When I tell my fellow passengers, they shoot me a glance that contains a mixture of surprise, pity, and envy. Italy is a boot-shaped mystery, and everybody, at least once in his or her lifetime, has thought about traveling the whole length of the country, to investigate.

Why am I doing this? Because I realized that I have never done it before. I've crossed Europe, America, Siberia, and Australia by train, not my own country. I've been almost everywhere in Italy, but there was no pattern. An assignment, a vacation, a short trip, a wedding, a visit to a friend or a relative—I've seen hundreds of individual places. But I never took the time to cross my own country. So I decided to do it, slowly, taking my time, watching the ever-changing land of Italy. I'll forget I'm a professional journalist, this time. Not an in-depth investigation, just a little taste of what I've been missing.

"I travelled among unknown men," wrote William Wordsworth. He came across them "in lands beyond the sea"; I'm going to meet them on a train in my own country, which—believe me—can be just as mysterious.

What is Italy? Is it an inferno, as some suspect, or a demon-speckled paradise? I'd say it was a pretty-looking purgatory, full of contented, tormented souls. The train is the perfect place to meet with them, listen to them, talk to them, understand what makes them tick. I'll be traveling before an election, which will contribute some tension to the travelers' mood. But, in Italy, politics is only background noise. We've seen so much for too long—rulers from Rome, from Greece, from Africa, from Germany and America; imperious priests and pious emperors; departing crusaders and incoming invaders; politicians of every shape and kind, from the Borgias to Berlusconi—to be overwhelmed by politics and politicians. At times they can be annoying, of course. But you get used to them, and you go on with your life.

Regional Express no. 2210 rolls quietly westward. Nicola and Alice—the cowboy and the squaw—exchange a kiss as we pass the Castle of Miramare, beautiful and spooky, built for Archduke Ferdinand Maximilian of Austria. The feathers in her headdress, backlit by the pale blue of the sea, are spectacularly out of place.

It's the last day of carnival. There is a sensation that something is coming to an end. In Venice, at the Santa Lucia station—snow and salt on the ground, water the color of steel—not even the masked partyers look all that cheerful. The performance of fun, but nothing more. A gust of young women in eighteenth-century garb blows by, greeting us as they pass. Students at the Academy of Fine Arts of Venice offer to face-paint passersby for five euros apiece. "So you see what I studied for?" says Michela, who comes from Brescia.

Young people in costume walk seriously past, and a group of undersized Asians pushes oversized suitcases through the piles of snow. It's damp and cold. I go back into Santa Lucia railway station. We pull out again. Eleven days to go, at my chosen slow pace. Sicily is more than a thousand miles away.

Mantua–Genoa

Mantua is situated in a bay in the sea of grass of Lombardy. The railway station is a frozen anchorage, and it's not uncommon to have to spend more time there than scheduled. Here Trenord (the northern network) meets Trenitalia (the national network), and the results are occasionally bizarre. Indeed, we miss the regional train for Cremona—we don't even see it pull out; Track 5 is hidden somewhere. Stefano Scansani, a local journalist and a friend, jokes about the rail-replacement bus service: the contract, he says, was assigned in a competition to a company from Puglia, five hundred miles from here. None of the drivers are familiar with the area, and when the fog is especially thick, they ask the passengers for directions. But all too often the passengers aren't even Italian; they're guest workers from Africa, and they haven't a clue either.

Some Italians are on this train, though. They inform me that yesterday the factory workers at the Burgo paper mill, slated to be shut down soon, evicted the HR director, carrying his desk and office furniture out into the snow. The local farmers' bank has problems; the chemical industry is struggling; the owners of the Mantua soccer team, Mantova FC, want to sell. The Camera degli Sposi (Wedding Room) in the Ducal Palace, one of the leading local tourist attractions, has been closed since the earthquake of 2012. True, Mantua hosts Festivaletteratura, the best literary festival in Europe. But it's not enough to uplift the residents' mood.

The train for Modena leaving at 11:31 a.m. is slow, clean, and painted with nursery school hues (lemon yellow, sky blue, pea green). Hares leap happily across snowbound fields. Between Mantua and Modena most of the passengers are recent immigrants. A few university students board at stations with intensely literary names and sprawl in their seats, earbuds in their ears and books in their arms. We pull into Modena fifteen minutes behind schedule, and I miss our connection. Two trains missed in half a day: not bad.

I board the 1:41 p.m. heading for Piacenza. The city, known across Italy for its superb *coppa* ham, offers a chilly welcome: this is a matter not of hospitality, but of temperature. My fellow passengers are actually nice and quite happy to talk. This is not unusual. Italy's trains are places of group confession and collective absolution, which is ideal for a Catholic country. Foreigners should listen to what people are saying. If they don't speak Italian, they can watch how they gesture. It's performance art. Do you think that confessionals and stages are incompatible? In other countries, they might be, but not here. The conversations are public exhibitions, with their own rituals and virtuoso touches.

Look at those three. They could be colleagues returning from a business meeting. They're not talking; they're proclaiming. They're not communicating; they're issuing mini-communiqués, drafted by the mini media offices each of them has in his or her head. As you can hear, they're arguing. And revealing some quite amazing details. They tackle one topic after another, piling arguments—and voices—on top of one another. Actually, the train is the precursor of the talk show. It offers a set, a backdrop, personalities, and various ways to make your exit.

I leave Piacenza aboard the regional train no. 20388 at 3:15 p.m., heading west to Voghera: subtropical temperature inside the train, snow as far as the eye can see outside. Voghera or Volgograd? one is tempted to ask. The train compartment conversation—the kind that leads people to confide—is absent; the compartment-less open space of a local train car tends to induce short questions and monosyllabic responses—you know everybody can hear you. In Voghera, while waiting for our train, two solidly built women in their early forties tell us they're from Liguria and every day they spend more than two hours commuting by train. Together, we board the Intercity no. 673, which arrives in Genoa twenty minutes late. Yesterday morning we were in Trieste; just two days later we've reached another sea. Haven't heard much about mood.

Genoa–Livorno

The dark-haired young woman is called Esmeralda and she looks suspiciously at my notebook. After a while she lets her hair down and starts to talk. She was a contestant on *Uomini e Donne*, a reality show on Italian television. She did it for fun, she tells me. She's now dating another contestant. She's going to see him in Rome for Valentine's Day. Signorina Esmeralda's political program is fairly simple: "Send all of them out to work in the fields. That way they will get an understanding of the value of hard work!" A buzz of approval in the compartment on the Intercity no. 511 Turin–Salerno, which has just pulled out of Genoa.

Intercity no. 511 is an age-old train of domestic migration, and it preserves all the character of its tradition. A fascinating Italian blender, capable of bringing together geography, income, education, and history. The drinks cart dodges around suitcases, dogs, and children. It isn't the modern drinks cart of the high-speed train from Milan to Rome and Naples. It's the epitome of an old-fashioned railway drinks cart, pushed by an attendant with a cap and a certain difficulty when it comes to making change. The announcement comes not from a loudspeaker but from a pair of weary lips that have uttered the words too many times: "Ice-cold Coca-Cola! Beer! Sandwiches, potato chips, espresso!" I eye the good old TUC crackers in their yellow packaging: a reassuring presence. The world changes, but TUC doesn't.

In Liguria I ask for opinions about the upcoming election and a local boy, Beppe Grillo, the founder of the populist Five Star Movement. And opinions are forthcoming. I'll confess: I was expecting greater enthusiasm. The caustic mistrust intrinsic to the Ligurian character clearly doesn't spare even its famous sons.

Anna Maria thinks the Five Star Movement will win, but she has no intention of contributing to it with her own vote. Nor will Mr. Grillo get the vote of Stefano, a student majoring in economics: he doesn't like the fact that Grillo refuses to participate in televised debates. Franco, having run through a litany of complaints about the bathrooms aboard this train, opines that in Genoa, the more traditional parties aren't doing all that badly. Elio and Angela, an argumentative couple, don't understand why Beppe Grillo doesn't run for office himself, but instead only sends the others on ahead. To summarize: polls say the Five Star Movement is popular in Liguria, but not aboard the Intercity no. 511.

There's nothing heroic about riding the length of Italy from north to south in a second-class seat; still, it's good for you. A train compartment induces conversation, and the confinement of the place reveals a lot about Italy. American students, instead of spending a semester in foreigners-packed Florence, should board a train like this, and listen.

The mysterious disappearance of three carriages this morning, and the renumbering of the remaining ones, with resulting chaos in the numbered seating, would have caused a hysterical fit if the passengers were from northern Europe. Not so among the Italians, who today, here, in our presence, struggle to make up for the ineptitude of Trenitalia, dealing with double-booked seats and immense suitcases. They look at one another, they inquire, and they offer advice and console one another. "If you only knew, my dear signore . . . !" "Don't worry, signorina. Let me help you with this."

A pair of Neapolitans—mother and daughter—read *Diva e Donna*, a women's magazine. They travel with flowers and shopping bags, tell me that they're fans of Silvio Berlusconi, and decide to take responsibility for my nourishment: small panini appear with cubes of pancetta, focaccia with herbs, and tangerines. Outside, in the sun, the steep slopes of Liguria fall away as we near Tuscany. The conductor has a weary, philosophical expression. He confesses his undying love for these old compartments, but he's perplexed by the geography of the railways along this coast of Italy: "The tunnels are small—they seem like they've been here forever. Every so often I look at them and wonder, will we be able to fit into them and get back out?"

I'm tempted to tell him that's the same question that we all ask ourselves all the time, for the whole of Italy. Will we get out of the tunnel? But it's best not to overthink it and just keep going.

Livorno–Perugia

Livorno is a city that is rarely given its due. It's open to the sea and to political arguments, both of which are fascinating things. A taxi driver remembers when he used to climb on his motorcycle and set out for Trieste with a thermos full of *ponce* (pronounced more or less like *punch*), a beloved local alcoholic concoction; he comes close to tears. Livorno witnessed the founding of the Italian Communist Party in 1921. The city is leftist by personality and history, the perfect place to ask all those who don't flee at the sight of a notebook, what do they think of Matteo Renzi, the wonder boy of Italian left-wing politics, born and bred here in Tuscany?

We walk into the station, where the *Regionale Veloce* no. 3114 awaits us. The first adjective (regional) is undeniable, because we're going to Florence, which is in the same region; as for the second one (*veloce*, or fast), we might reasonably argue some of the finer points. Says a young woman who is an office worker and a commuter: "Matteo Renzi? The former mayor of Florence? The left wing I like is quite different, the left wing that doesn't privatize a city's public transportation system!" The second young woman, who studies architecture, says: "I don't know if I'll be voting for Matteo Renzi's party, but I'll vote!" The third young woman, age nineteen, works as a barista in Pisa, and she asks: "Who's Matteo Renzi?"

We pull into the station of Santa Maria Novella. Standing in front of the departures board—nose in the air, hands in his pockets—is Signor Cornini. Impossible to miss him: floppy hat, rumpled jacket, he looks like a British country squire, just back from the hunt. He's a banker by profession, and when we ask him his opinion about Italian politics, he snaps: "When it comes to failing state-owned companies, the left lacks courage!" Then he looks up to see whether the departure for his train is going to pop up, like a quail on a foggy moor.

Trains are a soft drug: you quickly get used to these temporary acquaintanceships, these people who confide without consequences, the mechanical and psychological pitch and roll. What the British love about trains is their predictability: they wait for them to go by at level crossings (they call it trainspotting); they study the timetables and appreciate the rituals (these are rail buffs). Nothing about an Italian train, in contrast, is predictable. No one ever does what you might expect. The shyest passenger, once prodded to speak, proves to be a motormouth;

the toughest woman turns out to be solicitous and kind. Conductors don't ask why I interview fellow passengers. Their expressions tell me: "Anyone who travels by train for ten days listening to anyone is a hero, a masochist, or a lunatic. In any case, he deserves our sympathy."

Matteo Renzi is a good topic of conversation. In Tuscany, you need only say the name and you're bound to prompt reactions: passionate or argumentative, full of support or sarcasm, never indifference. The most common sentiment, even among those who wouldn't have voted for him, is regret—the election would have been more interesting with him in it. A great many say the same thing: he's *un bischero nuovo* (a new jerk, using the distinctively Tuscan term *bischero*). Instead we're condemned to the same old thing; and Tuscany is as allergic to boredom as cats are to water.

Perugia—L'Aquila—Pescara

I read in Michael Kerr's *Last Call for the Dining Car* that a reader wrote to the *Daily Telegraph* in praise of late trains and justifying the high prices: "The purpose of railways is not to convey people as quickly as possible from A to B, but rather to recall modern man from his headlong rush to nowhere by providing him with a time-opportunity to consider whether his journey from cradle to shroud is worthwhile. As Mr. T. S. Eliot has observed: 'You are not the same people who left that station / Or who will arrive at any terminus.' The railways are one of the few remaining English institutions that provide such an opportunity for reflection—and who would begrudge an extra pound for such an invaluable public service?"

It would be interesting to read this quotation aloud at Perugia Centrale station, at eight forty-five in the morning, while the vending machine refuses to spit out the ticket (though it's taken the money for it), and Signor Beniamino Cenci Goga, who introduces himself as "monarchist and Marxist," inquires politely about my destination.

Maybe Italy will never change, but I'm certainly going to. Today: Perugia, Foligno, and Terni in Umbria; Rieti in Lazio; L'Aquila, Sulmona, and Pescara in Abruzzi. While waiting for my first connecting train, I meet Ernesto, twenty-three years old, parka and backpack, law student. He's about to set off on a nine-hour trip to Brindisi, and his departure is already delayed by half an hour. "Trapani? By train? You're nuts. You'd be better off hitchhiking."

The problem isn't just getting south: it's getting *across*. Cutting horizontally across Italy, seated inside a railway car, is a form of heroism. The main railroads run along Italy's length from north to south, and follow the Adriatic and Tyrrhenian coasts. Between them lie the Apennines, the country's impervious spine. But the diesel locomotive ALn668 with manual transmission offers plenty of consolations: it passes over the snowy peaks, skirts around sheer crags, and slips through tiny tunnels. Italy, between Umbria and upper Lazio, seems to be a model railroad. Aboard the minitrain, in the bright February light, there are six passengers, including me. A solitary Brazilian woman. A little boy who obstinately keeps trying to slam against the door separating the two train cars. His mother, who keeps trying to dissuade him from it. On the right side, colorful graffiti obstructs the view from the bottom half of the windows; anyone who wishes to look out and see Umbria sliding away toward Rieti, standing room only.

At Rieti a medical student boards the train, dressed as Beau Brummell and heading for L'Aquila. On Monte Giano, in the distance, the trees have been planted so as to form an immense sign reading DUX, a scary reference to Benito Mussolini. It's a family-run little train; they even let us get footage of the driver's compartment. We reach L'Aquila, heralded by the so-called "new towns," set on cement legs, like colorful insects. Faithful to the railway inspiration of this journey, I won't be leaving the station. I'll stay here and ask about the earthquake of 2010, the reconstruction, and the recovery that doesn't seem to be happening.

Roberto, barista: "My grade for the reconstruction? An F. Nothing but a face-lift. Go take a look at what the 'new towns' really are—they're full of cracks and holes." Bruno, recently back from America: "We should bring back Berlusconi! They've had it up to here around these parts. Everyone's stressed out. Where I live, there's no work, not so much as a wheelbarrow in sight!" Mario, train conductor: "The first thing? Logistics and services. Otherwise this city is done for. There's nothing left downtown." Giovanna, maintenance worker: "Jobs for the young, or else they'll all just leave. My grade to the government for the reconstruction? I'd give them a D."

Another diesel-powered minitrain, the Maiella Mountains ahead of us, then the Aterno River valley, and Sulmona. Train station cafés shape travelers' moods. Nothing can shake the equanimity of those who look on, under neon fluorescent light, as an Abruzzese finger sandwich takes a Ligurian name, or the other way around. But in Sulmona the female barista, queen of her domain of scratch-and-win tickets and chocolate bars, is in a cheerful frame of mind. A young man comes over and, for unknown reasons, swears. She asks him to shut up, and he does.

We pull out. Abruzzo rolls past, as we descend toward the Adriatic, and the country changes its mood. The eastern, Adriatic side of the Italian boot may not be as spectacular as the western, Tyrrhenian side, but it's jollier. Gangs of eighteen-year-olds head to Silvi Marina. When I ask them to confirm the name of the station we see approaching, they shout in chorus: "Pescara!" As they get out under the station's bright lights, they seem content. And they're right: it's an Italian Saturday night, after all.

Pescara—Foggia—Benevento

Boarding the Frecciabianca no. 9803 for Foggia, after two days of back and forth aboard regional trains between Livorno and Pescara, is like going from a rowboat to a cabin cruiser. A tray table! A spacious seat! Only limited noise! A clean window! Stunned by all the luxury, in the calm of a railway car on Sunday, I open my newspaper and read about political corruption, scandals, sentencings, escapades of all sorts. Then I look at the faces around me in second class: everyone knows about this state of affairs, but they don't look angry about it. Not good.

We left the station at 12:40 p.m. There were no trains available earlier in the day, and that proved to be an advantage. Pescara is worth exploring, and Sunday morning is the ideal time for that. It's a city on the sea that never forgets it's on the sea; a city aided by geography and inclined to fantasy. Two great, unusual Italian writers, Gabriele D'Annunzio and Ennio Flaiano, are both from here. Pescara is a charming "P Town"; like its alphabetical sister towns—Perugia, Pisa, Pistoia, Parma, Piacenza, Pavia, Padua—it has known its ups and downs, and yet it has everything it needs to be happy. Low profile, medium size, high potential. A good place to visit if you want to know Italy. Pescara offers the right mix of mild unpredictability and sensory reassurance that is Italy's trademark. A town like this is far from perfect—some of the new housing on the seashore is pretty ugly, to be honest. But it represents the stunning, ordinary charm of the country better than our world-famous art cities. Rome, Venice, and Florence are unique and breathtaking: they intimidate you. Pescara takes you by the hand and slowly teaches you what Italy is about. It's smiles and waterways, lush greenery and lighthearted conversation, seafood served by old, ceremonious waiters, and lovely breakfasts in Corso Umberto.

The train rolls down the Adriatic coast; it enters Molise, Italy's second-smallest region. The sea is blue-gray; the empty white *stabilimenti balneari*, as the paying beach clubs are called, await better days. Sirena Beach, Bagni Blutur, then the city of Termoli: another *T* in this trip from Trieste to Trapani. Dunes, beaches, maritime pines. Everything becomes more spacious, calmer, different. Around here, invisibly, we cross the border to the South.

The Gargano Promontory appears through the mist, beyond flat fields and vineyards. We arrive in Foggia, which I recently visited as a guest of a high school. I think of the impressive students I met and the strange fate of the Italian South: unless these cities clean up and change, the young people won't stay; if the young people won't stay, these cities won't change. An odd Mediterranean catch-22, a trap we should try to find a way out of.

I decide to buttonhole the entire carriage no. 7 of train no. 9354 for Benevento for an impromptu opinion poll: how's Italy doing? The level of tolerance for this unasked-for buttonholing is high; the percentage of abstention is low. Nicola, age thirty-six, believes that the real gap isn't between generations, but between well-informed people and unin-formed people. Francesca is traveling with her husband and two chil-dren to Rome, where she goes periodically for medical treatment. She hopes things will pick up, but she's not counting on it. When she talks about her family's problems, with her daughter in her arms, she doesn't feel angry. She feels sad. "I don't want to give up," she says.

We enter Campania, the twelfth region of this trip, and pull into Benevento, midway between the Tyrrhenian Sea and the Adriatic Sea. In the station, policemen and nuns in the wilderness of Sunday. Just outside the station, posters that seem to have been there forever. "The Economic Downturn Is Extinguishing Nightlife in the Center of Town," announces the local edition of *Il Mattino*. "More Bankruptcies and Fewer Divorces: Blame It on the Economic Downturn" is the head-line in *Il Sannio*. Business is shaky and more people are staying married because they can't afford to split up, in other words. Not good news for the battered Italian South.

Benevento–Bari–Taranto

I've developed a certain dislike for Uncle Giuseppe, continually men-tioned in the phone calls that my across-the-aisle neighbor is conduct-ing from Benevento to Bari. Audio spammers such as this guy are everywhere among us. They call five relatives, four colleagues, all sorts of old friends. These aren't urgent phone calls, just a way of passing the time and annoying one's neighbors.

Better mannered and far more interesting, it turns out, is Pablo, a toy poodle bred-in-the-bone native of Bari. The trip proceeds loquaciously—if Uncle Giuseppe is in need of a biographer, we're certainly up to the task—and Bari awaits us in the sunshine. Palm trees, the ocher yellow train station, dark-haired, quick-stepping women, the usual policemen everywhere. Standing on the platform, erect and solitary as a figure by Magritte, is a gentleman named Enzo. He introduces himself as an advertising executive with offices in Milan, London, and Padua, an expert in "Jungian psychometric processes." I cannot bring myself to tell him I don't know what he's talking about.

My next train departs from the "truncated Taranto track" situated between Track 3 and Track 4. A sort of Track 3½. In order to know that, though, you'd have to be Harry Potter. The directions are vague; the suitcases are bulky. I get there just as the conductor starts waving his arms and yelling, "Come on! Come on!"

After Acquaviva delle Fonti and Gioia del Colle—"Live Water from the Springs," "Happiness of the Hill"; the place-names of Puglia are poetic—the regional train no. 3163 heads down to the Ionian Sea through olive groves, vineyards, deep skies, and flat roofs. The train is short, clean, colorful, and efficient; at the center of each car, it offers charming seating areas complete with bow windows. It was purchased with funds from the European Union, a young man informs me.

The immense Ilva steel mill in Taranto suddenly looms up on our left. It is Italy's—and Europe's—largest steelworks. It employs eleven thousand people in the area. But it turned out to be an environmental nightmare. It has long been suspected of killing off local people by belching into the air a mix of minerals, metals, and carcinogenic dioxins. Shut it down or keep it open? A young lawyer explains: "It's like being asked to choose between your health and your job; no one is willing to make that choice." An out-of-towner who works in the city: "Ilva is a harmful presence here. But shutting it down would do even more harm." A voice rings out from the back of the passenger car: "Around here, nobody talks about anything but Ilva!" Rosa Salemme listens to us: "I've been breathing the air of Taranto for twenty-seven years. We consider Ilva to be something inevitable, but we need to start imagining an alternative. Go to the Tamburi neighborhood—it's right at the foot of the smokestacks: the whole place is orange."

Tamburi is in Taranto; we're arriving from Trieste and heading for Trapani: the T-junctions are starting to become quite numerous.

Taranto–Reggio Calabria

In eight days the train has carried me from Trieste all the way here, on the Ionian Sea, right under the sole of the Italian boot. Metaponto, in Basilicata, is proud of its new train station: five tracks, a renovation project that received financing to the tune of eighteen million euros from the European Union. But only one train comes through here a day, the Intercity for Rome: it drops me off at 8:21 in the morning, and from then on, it's my tough luck—or rather, my tough bus. If you want to travel farther south, to Calabria and Sicily—as I do—you have to take a replacement bus.

But who says that trains are indispensable to the successful operation of a railway station? In the bar of Metaponto railway station, I meet local farmers, who produce magnificent artichokes, spinach, and eggplants, vegetables that might reach central and northern Italy by train, the way they once did; instead, they contribute to traffic jams on the highways. Not even this is enough to change the mood of the clientele. This morning they are talking about taxes. They have a sense of humor in Basilicata—they refuse to admit that tax evasion is a serious problem in Italy. Actually they would like the proposal to liberalize the use of cash. "If money doesn't circulate, blood doesn't circulate!" says Mario, a farmer.

From Metaponto to Sibari, as I said, I find myself trainless. I travel aboard the Substitute Bus BA506, which is momentarily halted in its tracks in Trebisacce, outside the By Armentano clothing store, owned by the Armentano brothers (up to fifty percent off). The bus arrives on Viale della Libertà, finds a car double-parked, and has to wait. But the driver decides that our extremely tight connection in Sibari—a five-minute window—constitutes a point of honor for him. And in spite of city traffic, he keeps his promise. At 11:40 a.m. I board regional train no. 3727 to Catanzaro Lido. I talk politics with Rosy, a retired journalist, and Marco, forced to take the train because his license has been revoked. When I ask him, as a joke, which way to the restaurant car, he has momentary doubts about my mental health. It's easier to find a dinosaur than a restaurant car on a train in Calabria.

In the last section, from Catanzaro Lido to Reggio Calabria, I encounter a great many students: courteous young men with beards, lovely young women as dark as Byzantine Madonnas. Blue sea beneath the train window, so close that the self-propelled Littorina railcar seems to be racing over an empty beach. Clean bathroom facilities, no food whatsoever, tropical heating. I wonder whether the shortcomings of the Calabrian transportation system are the subject of discussions for travelers on this line. They are. "Politicians haven't kept the promises they made before, so they avoid making any new ones," says Consolato, disconsolately. "Promises about the transportation system? I don't think so," confirms Lucia, born in 1989. Protest? Not really. "You know how it is—we're traditionalists around here."

Right after passing through Locri, the little train comes to a sudden stop. Excited voices inform us: "We hit a sheep!" The conductor explains the reason for the unexpected stop: "We need to check the running gear." So it's a question not of the woolly fellow's health (needless to say, the sheep is no longer numbered among the living), but of the wheels and the brakes. When we get moving again, a robust-looking seventy-year-old sits down, gazes intensely at me, and asks, "So, what do you do?" I'm a journalist, I reply. "For what party?" For a newspaper, I explain. "But what party do you sympathize with?"

"I can tell you who I antipathize with."

"All right," he says.

We arrive in Reggio Calabria at 4:50 p.m., nine hours of travel since my departure from Taranto. The city is without a mayor: the government has been ousted from power since October, and the city placed under temporary receivership because of the mountain of debts it's struggling under. I'd like to know more, but I'm not in the mood to talk about local politics. I'll look at the winter sea, instead. Today it is smooth and turquoise, and Sicily is a green shadow on the horizon. Italy along its edges, I must say, always has a certain allure.

Reggio Calabria–Messina–Catania

Anyone who works for the railways in Calabria, when referring to the lines along the Ionian coast, speaks of "our Gaza Strip." An unruly place, let's say. Stopped cars on level crossings, passengers without tickets, teenage boys who pull the emergency brake to get out wherever they please. As I was saying, I was lucky: crystal clear sea, on-time performance, plenty of smiles. But the color of the Ionian and the friendly expressions may be sufficient for occasional passengers—not those who are forced to the daily routine.

The risk of the picturesque is considerable on this magnificent, troubled end of the Italian line. Many foreigners fall into it. But I'm no foreigner; I just come from far away in Italy. My hometown, Crema, is 68 miles from Switzerland and 762 miles from here.

Today's timetable includes a regional train from Reggio Calabria to Villa San Giovanni, then an Intercity, which will be loaded onto the ferryboat to Messina, and from there, on to Catania. Sicily—the sixteenth and last region of our trip—awaits me.

Regional train to Rosarno departing at 1:55 p.m.: standing room only until Villa San Giovanni. Here I discover that the Intercity no. 723 is running an hour late. I find an alternative, I cross the strait—where Ulysses lost six men battling the sea monster Scylla, and every Italian government, sooner or later, announces it will build a bridge—and I land in Sicily. I push my wheeled suitcase from the Messina ferry station to the railway station—for some mysterious reason the two are not connected—and I notice I will have to wait an hour and a half for the regional train. Why are there no connections with the ferry from mainland Italy? It's a mystery. The station is big, empty, and vaguely cemetery-like. Approaching people seems pointlessly cruel.

But traveling in Italy—in southern Italy, in particular, and most especially in Sicily—is always the source of surprises. Hermes, a journalism student, introduces himself and tells me that he wrote his thesis on the political connivances in the media in Messina. I congratulate him, as there are plenty of connivances between politics and the media, in Messina and in the whole of Sicily. He smiles, and unpacks a tray full of truly majestic cannoli.

Regional train no. 3869 departs on time, at 4:20 p.m. The sky is dark. Santa Teresa di Riva, Giardini Naxos, Acireale: the coast is magnificent, and we can just glimpse it between the low clouds and the steel gray sea. Traveling with us are twenty French students from the agronomy school of Clermont-Ferrand. A study trip, I am told. I ask, "How is your stay? Do you understand Italian politics?" A young woman opens her eyes wide: "In France, there is real tension around politics! Here we hardly noticed it." Then she introduces me to Margaux, the class mascot, a plush monkey. I look at the monkey carefully, as darkness falls over Sicily: there are politicians with less personality.

Catania–Palermo

It's hard to tell the story of an empty day: empty of events, passengers, conversations. But this is an island full of surprises, and on our railway trip from Trieste to Trapani, we must tell what we found. Today, that was little or nothing. In front of the Catania station, the gelato van catches a whiff of poor business to come. Inside, at the ticket window, Salvatore tries to keep up his morale: "Here people don't have much of a culture of the train. They go to Palermo by bus or by car. Because, let's admit it: the schedules are inconvenient, and not all the trains are like this one."

Sicily without light is unrecognizable. We leave Catania in the early afternoon beneath an ominous deep gray sky, in an unnatural calm. It will soon bring a very violent cloudburst—city flooded, cars submerged, pedestrians swept away—but the regional train no. 3853 gets out ahead of it, just slips under it, and heads inland. An impeccable, spotless, punctual train, the only one for Palermo; deserted, though. If Trenitalia knew my destination and schedule in advance—it does not—I'd suspect that these cars had been curated for the naive travel writer. Instead I discover that the regional train is always like this: decorous, clean. And empty.

There are eight of us, engineer and conductor included. The cars—light blue and silent—look like the locker rooms of a swimming pool during a swimming lesson. Our train climbs toward Enna and runs through an enchanting landscape: green, uneven, low mountains and scattered houses. To kill time, and to give the passengers something to do, I go to the central seating area—conveniently arrayed in a small amphitheater—and convene a council of cabinet ministers. Let everyone choose an area of responsibility, and say the first thing they would do to improve things in Italy! My fellow passengers look at me as if I am crazy. Then they say, why not?

After a brief argument over who will get to be the minister of transportation, the discussion begins, under the amused gaze of the conductor. Antonella, a student majoring in history at Messina, chooses the Ministry of Education: she wants money for scholarships and schools that aren't falling apart. Salvatore T., our minister of transportation, says he belongs to the "big family of the Italian railways." He's thinking of high-speed rail in Sicily, but he's afraid that it might come to nothing, like the bridge over the strait. Salvatore D., former CPA, is the most enthusiastic: he chooses the Ministry of the Treasury and asks to be made the minister of outlays. He'd be the right one to calculate the waste, he says with grim satisfaction.

The train stops at the station at Enna (empty) and Caltanissetta Xirbi (deserted); only at Termini Imerese, on the coastline again, does anybody board the train. The conductor, in regulation jacket and jeans, isn't happy: in Sicily, given the regional government's well-known financial difficulties, many local services have been cut, and there's a real danger that this train line will meet the same fate. "Everyone wants to drive; it's always more cars! We want to leave from our front door and park right where we're going, even if it means triple-parking." We who? I ask. We Italians? He looks at me in surprise: "We Sicilians!"

We pull into Palermo five minutes late: no sign with the name of the city, for some reason. Cool evening, yellow lights. The newly appointed minister of outlays, faithful to his mandate, shows us the way out of the station. A young woman in a heavy jacket notices me, breaks away from her four friends. She's seen me on television. She orders me to ask her a question. I toss out: "We decided to take the train from Catania. Did we do the right thing?" "From Catania? By train?" She bursts into a convulsion of laughter.

If that's a welcome to Palermo, I like it. It's nice to see someone in a cheerful mood, once in a while.

Palermo–Trapani

I left from Trieste; today I'll arrive in Trapani, the end of the line of my railway journey, from the far northeast to the far southwest of a worried nation. The regional train no. 8605 departs Palermo station at 9:29 a.m. It's the last day, so I decide to trouble the other travelers immediately.

Palermo is every bit as ancient and skeptical as the island it represents, and it can't be upset by a traveling writer and his political questions. Over the years, it has passed from the center to the left to the
right—and back, of course. My fellow passengers are cordial; they don't
run away at the sight of my notebook. A Northerner with a suitcase
asking political questions first thing in the morning is strange, and
around here, strangeness is considered an added value. We spend an
hour discussing parties, leaders, promises, and disappointment. Sicilians are masters of language. In the end, I don't know what they really
think. But they all seem satisfied. They've been kind to an outsider
without committing themselves. After all, you never know who might
win the election.

The train is full of light and it has a charming name: Minuetto.
This rail line was opened in 1937. The previous one between Palermo
and Trapani, inaugurated by the Società della Ferrovia Sicula
Occidentale—Western Sicilian Railway Company—in 1885, passed
through Mazara and Marsala; the total distance was 194 kilometers—120
miles—and the trip took ten hours. The point of the operation wasn't
to take passengers to Trapani, but to convey the wines of Marsala and
the seafood of Mazara to Palermo. Even today, passenger service
doesn't seem to be a particular priority. Not even to the passengers,
who—as we have seen—will gladly take a bus or their own car whenever possible.

Lucia, twenty-four, is also heading back to Trapani. She studies on
the train, book perched on her knees. She explains how difficult it is to
navigate the murky waters of the University of Palermo toward her
degree. She tells of exams rescheduled without notification, long waits
in department hallways, mercurial professors. ("If they take an instant
dislike to you, then it's tough. The last one yelled at me, right in my
face. It was that way from day one.") "And in the psychology department, things are pretty good. In literature and business, things are even
worse." Disappointed? "Look: if you get your degree at Palermo, it

means you really wanted to study. But it's sad. It is as if my generation doesn't exist."

Stormy skies along the way: the train windows look like Turner paintings. I departed from Trieste, and I'm arriving in Trapani after eleven days of travel, about thirteen hundred miles, sixteen regions, thirty stations, twenty-seven trains, and a replacement-railway bus. The trip ends with the sea on my right, green fields on my left, surrounded by ruins, prickly pears, overpasses, and lemon trees. I've watched thousands of Italians, listened to a few hundred. Do I know who is going to win this election? Of course not, but that was not the purpose of my journey. I crossed my country by land, from the border with Slovenia to a place where on a clear day you can see Africa, to check if we're still one nation. We are, I must say. From north to south, people want a good job, a good family, good friends, and some happiness on the side. A better government? That, too. But not enough people are ready to give up their old habits and their little privileges in order to improve the quality of public life. Therefore Italy stays the same: an emotional, maddening proving ground and a great temptation. We are what others would like to be—at least some of the time— but don't dare try.

7

Trans–Siberian Express: Honeymoon for Four

1986

What you are reading was written in a notebook crowded among two teaspoons, a soup spoon, a bottle of Russian mineral water, a packet of hand wipes, and three used tea bags that Lyuba refuses to take away. Here I should be more precise, because there are two Lyubas: the one who refuses to take away the tea bags is Big Lyuba, and when she walks down the train car corridor, her hips dust the window and at the same time the compartment door. The other one is Little Lyuba, who smokes Marlboros and smiles at any man under thirty.

This is a confession: for our honeymoon I took my wife on a train trip of 5,593 miles in second class, which means with two strangers in the same compartment. In my defense, let me say (1) I'm not an idiot—I *had* reserved a first-class compartment so as to be alone with my bride, but the Russians screwed us; and (2) the Trans-Siberian Express is a dangerous temptation for a train lover: it runs across nearly one hundred degrees of longitude, as well as six time zones, and takes six days, one hour, and forty-one minutes. It leaves Moscow at 11:50 on Friday night and arrives in Beijing the following Friday at 6:31 in the morning. The food is terrible, you can only wash in the most rudimentary manner imaginable, the longest stop is for fifteen minutes, and the Russians do everything they can to convince you that you ought to have spent your vacation anywhere else but there. Still, it's a remarkable journey, and if your wife is still smiling when you reach Beijing station, she's an extraordinary woman, and you did the right thing by marrying her.

/////////////////

Trains heading for Siberia depart from the Yaroslavskaya station in Moscow, which you can guess by the people waiting. Sitting on the largest suitcases I've ever seen in my life, a horde of Tartars, Buryats, Koreans, Mongols, Kyrgyz, and Uzbeks, possibly accompanied by a few Russians, wait impassively under the fluorescent lights. They don't seem to be waiting for an imminent departure; they just look like they're waiting, period.

Our train sits on Track 5. It's green and looks like any ordinary train except for the magical sign reading Moscow–Beijing. An Englishman loaded down with cameras is informing a fellow traveler that the Trans-Siberian Express is the only overland connection between western Europe and the Pacific Ocean. The Russians are building a road, but it's not yet finished, and even once it is finished, it will always be less reliable than the railroad: you can clear snow more easily off two rails than off a roadway. I would have liked to go on listening, but my wife, who's already boarded the train, leans out the window and informs me that "there are four of us in the compartment, the bathroom is microscopic, and there's a radio blaring in Russian." We crack up laughing. What else can we do?

First Day

With us in the compartment are two young Russian women, who talk a great deal. The radio talks even more than they do, and nobody seems to know how to make it stop. As the train moves away from the station, leaving behind us the Tartars, Buryats, Mongols, and Uzbeks standing impassively under the fluorescent lights, we start exploring the carriages. We aren't allowed to go forward, into the cars where most Russians travel; Big Lyuba, one of the two female conductors, explains this to us, barring our way and teaching us the one fundamental phrase for anyone who wishes to understand the Soviet universe: *nye razreshayet-sya,* "not allowed." We turn around and head back, walking through first class, and then the dining car, and finally the cars occupied by the athletes of the North Korean national team, on their way home from the "Goodwill Games" in Moscow. Traveling in first class are six Swedish couples bursting with health, one couple per compartment, even though they're not on their honeymoon. In the dining car sits a man named Boris, with a tie that he must have cooked in many different sauces. He informs us of the breakfast schedule for the following morning.

In addition to their conductor duties, Lyuba and Lyuba are responsible for cleaning the cars. Our compartment is reasonably clean, at least. The two top bunks can be folded up flat against the wall during the day. Lowering the windows isn't hard, provided you have two people hanging off the handles. The tray table can be collapsed like on any other train, and it almost immediately proceeds to do so, spilling a cup of scalding tea onto the floor. There is a restroom at either end of the car. In order to wash, there's only a sink the size of half a watermelon, strictly without a stopper: if you want to fill the sink, you'll need a small rubber ball—which we brought with us, having been warned. Among the conductors' other tasks is to lock the bathroom doors ten minutes before pulling into stations and unlock them ten minutes after each departure. During the journey, I'll have an opportunity to see that the two Lyubas perform this duty with a zeal bordering on sadism: no amount of begging will sway them, no number of contortions outside the locked door.

As we delve into the mysteries of the restroom and struggle to silence the radio, the train rolls through the darkness toward Zagorsk, past the dachas of the Muscovites, and arrives at Yaroslavl at three in the morning. The fact that this city on the Volga was the terminus of the railroad around 1860, when the idea of the Trans-Siberian Express was first conceived, is not enough to get anyone out of their bunks. In the morning, after discovering that they serve salami and not much more for breakfast, I devote myself to the landscape: flat, green, no animals in sight, even though the *Atlas of the Soviet Union* claims that this is "a land of cattle and dairy products." In Danilov I make the acquaintance of several strapping representatives of the army of Soviet railroad workers (3.5 million employees), who in this circumstance are resupplying the train with water: elderly women, who in Italy would be spending the winter on the Riviera, but here leap from one track to another, brimming over with vim and vigor.

As the enormous Soviet forest streams past the windows—a quarter of all the trees on earth, larch trees as far as the eye can see—I discover on a shelf in the corridor various pamphlets meant for the travelers' political education: among the most interesting ones are *Contemporary Trotskyism Versus Peace and Détente* and *True and False Interests for the Rights of Man*, which cheer me up until we reach Kirov at one thirty in the afternoon. That city used to be called Vyatka, until Stalin renamed it after his friend Sergei Mironovich Kirov, perhaps to console himself for having had him killed. Toward evening, after crossing the river Kama, we reach Perm, 895 miles from Moscow. This city was called Molotov from 1940 until 1957, but since Soviet place-names are always a matter of opinion, Khrushchev changed the name back to Perm. We stop here for fifteen minutes. That's not much time, but it's more than enough for the North Koreans to ransack the station's kiosks: with badges featuring Kim Il-sung on their chests, they rush out all together and come back loaded down with *mineralnye vody* (mineral water) and moss-colored sandwiches.

Second Day

While we were sleeping, the train has taken a number of interesting initiatives. It's climbed over the Ural watershed; it's passed the obelisk eleven hundred miles from Moscow with EUROPE written on one side and ASIA on the other; it's entered a different time zone from the capital; and finally, it has stopped in Sverdlovsk. From here on, we're in Siberia, and we follow the *trakt*, the route that the czar's couriers rode from Saint Petersburg to Irkutsk, on the shores of Lake Baikal. We roll through ramshackle towns with dirt roads, few cars in sight, and only the occasional motorcycle with sidecar. We cross paths with the Rossiya, the red train that runs from Vladivostok, and an endless succession of freight trains—on average, one every two minutes—which bring lumber and minerals to Moscow, and whose diesel engines spill grimy dirt in through our windows. Thanks to that, but not only that, the compartments are starting to take on the lovely appearance of little stables. Even though we change our clothing every day and wash with the assistance of the little rubber ball, our cleanliness is rudimentary. Thanks to Lyuba and Lyuba, the two restrooms are always reasonably clean, though with every passing hour, the odor of the robust Russian air freshener becomes increasingly nauseating.

At eleven a.m., the train stops at Ishim, where it's drizzling, and then departs as usual without warning, obliging a crowd of loitering passengers to chase frantically after it. The landscape is becoming interesting. As Lyuba and Lyuba confirm with a military nod of the head, this is the steppe, where Siberia starts to get serious. Here the population is mostly Russian, but there are also enclaves of Kazakhs, Estonians, Ukrainians, Tartars, and Germans, the latter being soldiers in the Red Army whom Stalin chose to transport here from the Volga region, where their ancestors had settled at the invitation of Catherine the Great. Chekhov passed through here in 1890, aboard a horse-drawn tarantass, and was struck by the "black earth" and the "distinctive

Russian stench." We, too, see the black earth, and we get plenty of the
Russian stench from Boris's dining car, which we are obliged to visit
twice a day. There, a waiter with the appearance of a Polish count
pretends he has understood our orders, and then invariably brings us
salami and cucumbers.

At last, on the steppes of Ishim, we see livestock grazing. Cows, for
the most part, which must somehow have learned to survive the climate
of these places: snow on the ground for 150 days a year, an average
winter temperature of five degrees below zero, and hard frosts every
month of the year except for July and August. We cross the Barabinsk
steppe, a colossal expanse that runs from the fifty-third to the fifty-
seventh parallels north, and arrive in Novosibirsk, widely called the
Chicago of Siberia, at 2:25 a.m., a time of night when Siberian railway
stations don't offer a lot of amusements.

I try to take a picture of the engine, but I'm courteously invited to
cease and desist by Big Lyuba: trains, stations, and bridges, *nye razre-
shayetsya*. We pull out. Someone, in the darkness, claims to have seen
the river Ob.

Third Day

The morning is bright and sunny and the train climbs up into the
mountains. Finally, in the curves of the tracks, we are able to see the
whole train, from the engine to the very last car. It's almost hot out, and
little Russian girls, with their regulation hair bow, wait obediently in
the stations: Bogotol, where we arrive at seven in the morning; Achinsk,
where the train stops for three minutes, just long enough to admire the
local station, which in every way resembles an armor-plated diner.
Each time the ritual is identical: little uniformed men check the wheels
of the trains; passengers get out to stretch their legs, running back and
forth like drunken ants; a few people tarry to purchase raspberries—
one ruble a paper twist—and come dangerously close to missing the

train. After Krasnoyarsk, which we are told is much nicer than its station, the train crosses the Yenisey River, enormous and covered with rafts, and then pushes on into the taiga, the Siberian forest, which is teeming with insects in this season, including the *klesh*, a tick that causes encephalitis, and against whose bite all the inhabitants have been vaccinated. In the afternoon we reach Tayshet, the terminus of the BAM (Baikal–Amur Mainline), the railroad that leads directly to the Pacific, built at the behest of Stalin and at the cost of the lives of half a million unlucky wretches. Again today, unfortunately, the grim ritual of the evening repast is repeated, and every day Boris the restaurateur keeps moving it a little earlier, because he insists that the stomach follows the sun, and the sun doesn't follow Moscow time the way the clocks of all the stations do. Around four in the afternoon, we very sadly troop in procession toward the dining car, where the usual soup with yogurt awaits us, accompanied by the perpetual salami and cucumbers and an egg with peas: this vegetable first appeared at breakfast, and we won't shake it till the end of the trip. To drink, we can choose between sickly-sweet apple juice and salty mineral water. In spite of numerous attempts to bribe the waiter, no beer and no vodka are forthcoming. Those drinks seem to have been abolished aboard the Trans-Siberian Express after several unseemly episodes that took place some time ago (did someone dare try to seduce Big Lyuba? we wonder).

Fourth Day

At six in the morning we pull into Irkutsk, the capital of eastern Siberia, an educated and tolerant city, 3,225 miles from Moscow and 2,367 from Beijing. Many Russians get off here, dragging packages and children as they go, and among those who board the train is a powerfully built, extremely blond schoolteacher, heavily made-up and teetering on very high heels. Despite the early hour, she wants to speak in English, and even though no one asked her, she informs us that she is bound for the school at Ulan-Ude, on the other side of Lake Baikal. The lake appears once the woman finally stops talking, after two tunnels—the first ones since we left Moscow—guarded by soldiers. The train plunges downhill, runs along the lakeshore for a few hours, and then heads east again. It reaches Ulan-Ude at 2:42 p.m. Moscow time, but it's almost dark because local time is 8:42 p.m. Having dedicated the entire day to an experiment with time zones—stick to Moscow time as far as Irkutsk, then suddenly leap forward to local time—I'm vaguely agog. Before going to bed, I'm forced to suffer the Lyubas' latest low blow: in order to battle the smells in the restroom, where several dozen people have been taking turns for the past four days, they have drastically increased the quantity of Russian air freshener. The resulting aromatic cocktail is lethal; without bothering to wash, I'm in my bunk by 3:30 p.m. Moscow time, while the train rolls on through the darkness of the Transbaikal region.

Fifth Day

After Lake Baikal, everything changes: the mountains become hills, the faces in the stations become Asian—this is the land of the Buryats, who speak a variety of Mongolian—and Ulan Bator isn't far away. Only the party slogans on the roofs and walls are still the same, even more deeply stirring here than in Moscow. A short distance after Chita, our car is uncoupled from the Trans-Siberian Express proper, which continues on to Vladivostok and the Pacific. Our train instead heads south toward Manchuria, following the rails of what was once called the Chinese Eastern Railway. Even though five days of travel have broken the spirit of many passengers, a few continue to stand with great dignity at the windows; the Buryats ride by on horseback, the land is a rolling plain, and the houses have sheet metal roofs and firewood already stacked for the winter, which around here must be a serious proposition.

We arrive in Olovyannaya at 6:25 a.m. Moscow time, 12:25 p.m. local time, crouched on our seats: Lyuba and Lyuba are cleaning the compartment, and they refuse to vacuum around passengers' feet. Ortensia tells me, with a smile: *Don't expect me to do this when we get back home.* Somewhere near here, on the banks of the Onon River, Genghis Khan, son of a Mongol tribal leader named Yesugei, was born in 1162; eight hundred years later, the Soviets have managed to ruin the place.

I thought I'd seen the ugliest station on the Trans-Siberian Express, but Dauriya, where packs of stray dogs chase after carts on dirt roads, is worse than Olovyannaya, and Zabaykalsk is worse than Dauriya. Zabaykalsk is the border crossing, and here the Soviets give the greatest expression of their refinement in the art of irritating their fellow man: everyone has to wait for three hours, a thorough check of all luggage, and a "political check" of my books. When I ask them why they're doing a political check when we *leave* the USSR, instead of more logically checking when we enter, all I get in response is a bored glance. When I try to lower the windows, a soldier barks at me to raise them immediately. When I point out that it's hot in there, he says that doesn't matter. Having exchanged the rubles that are wanted by nobody anywhere else in the world, and having changed the wheels on the train because in China the track gauge is narrower than in Russia, we depart.

The North Koreans, who can tell they're getting closer to home and are therefore understandably depressed, have remained seated for three hours in a waiting room that's so horrible it becomes fantastic: stucco, high windows, flowered armchairs, the smell of mold, the usual Soviet television set as green as an aquarium, and a black-and-white photo exhibit on the province's economic success. Moscow is 4,142 miles away, but that's the spirit of the thing.

The Chinese are waiting for us at Manzhouli, and they seem to have agreed in advance to smile, all together and at once. The customs formalities would have been straightforward except that two young Americans don't have a Chinese entry visa, and the Russians don't want them back. The Chinese think it over for two hours, and then, still with smiles on their lips, they inform the Americans that they must buy two visas then and there at a price of about five hundred dollars apiece. The Americans complain loudly, but they pay. We depart again.

Our two Russian roommates by now have realized that Ortensia and I are on our honeymoon. But there's not much they can do—the train is full, and we must share this compartment all the way to Beijing. I sense they feel pity for us when they start talking in heavily accented English to each other, so we can understand them.

> **FIRST GIRL:** Hey, my friend! Why don't we go for a walk along the train?
>
> **SECOND GIRL:** Good idea, my friend! And we won't be back for at least half an hour!

So these poor bastards can have sex, I guess they mean. But when they leave, Ortensia and I hold hands across our beds and start to laugh—happy, as you can be only when you're in your twenties, and in love.

Sixth Day

The Chinese don't like station stops. We cross the northern part of Inner Mongolia without stopping; we cross the forty-eighth parallel; we descend toward Harbin; we cross the newly flooded Jilin province. Big Lyuba sits majestically in her post beside the restroom, where the sheer concentration of air freshener makes it possible to stay only briefly, while holding one's breath. Little Lyuba gazes dreamily out the window and thinks about the Soviet border guard for whom she had dolled herself up.

We arrive at Beijing at eight thirty in the morning, only two hours late. The most spectacular sight in the station is the crowd of twelve French passengers with backpacks slung over their shoulders, excitedly waiting to leave for Moscow. Boris the restaurateur, who still hasn't run out of peas, lurks in his galley, just waiting for them.

I look at my wife: she's still smiling.

8

From the Baltic to the Bosphorus: The Last Summer of Communism

1989: The Delights of the Repin Express

The idea is simple: board a train in Helsinki and get off at Istanbul, traveling the rails of Actually Existing Socialism. A trip of this sort means translating mysterious timetables, struggling with sleeping bunks that fold up like pocketknives, and, most of all, confronting state tourism office clerks, who are determined to persuade us that it's faster by plane. All of this while trying never to lose our tempers, and instead almost inevitably losing them: the trains of Eastern Europe, in fact, can't be reserved from the West, they travel packed to the gills, and they either have dining cars that ought to be reported to the World Health Organization or else simply don't have them. There are magnificent consolations, though: Bulgarian conductors who sing through the night, keeping the whole sleeping car wide-awake, a party of Russian smugglers, American tourists who buff the window glass for hours before realizing that the dirt is outside. You look for trains, in other words, but what you find is passengers. And around these parts, the passengers have plenty of stories to tell.

The journey begins at the Rautatieasema in Helsinki, one of the few stations on earth that deserves a visit even if you have no train to catch: it's a sort of art nouveau temple designed by the world-famous architect Eliel Saarinen, in front of which four stone colossi welcome travelers with a sad expression. I do happen to have a train to catch, though, and it's standing at Track 6, surrounded by the small crowd that always seems to gather every time a plane or a ship departs for a Communist country. Many of the passengers are lugging big cardboard boxes, which—based on the illustrations on the boxes—contain everything from a tape recorder to a vacuum cleaner to show off to their friends back home as precious treasures.

The express train no. 23 is heading for Leningrad, 275 miles away, beyond lakes and national borders. It's a Russian train, riding on broad Soviet tracks with a five-foot gauge, which the Finns have adopted to avoid complications. Next to it sits the express train for Joensuu, with the phrase *SELVÄÄ SÄÄTÖÄ* written on its side: six diaereses in just two words, probably a record even around here. My train is called the Repin Express, taking its name from the painter Ilya Yefimovich Repin (1844–1930), whose house is included on the Vladimir Ilych Lenin Slept Here tour offered by the Leningrad Intourist office. The passengers in car no. 1 are more interested in the furnishings of the compartments: a table that becomes a sink; a mini-wardrobe with six clothes hangers; two beds, even if this is a day trip. The train departs at 1:12 p.m., and immediately the cool air of a Finnish summer wafts in. Or at least it does until 1:15, when the Russian conductor comes through and with a faint smile fastens all the windows shut. "Air-conditioning," he says, as if it were a luxury that we don't deserve.

The Repin Express goes through Kouvola, where a gardening stationmaster has planted flowers in the shape of the initials *VR* (Valtion-rautatiet, or Finnish railways); then it cuts south of the lake region and pulls into Vainikkala, the Finnish border crossing, at 4:15 in the afternoon. It stops here for twenty minutes, and the passengers, keenly aware of the buffets that await them in the train stations of Russia, hurry to stock up on provisions, pushing past people struggling with baggage carts and dragging suitcases. Two American retirees from Vermont ask me, "We're entering Russia. Aren't you excited?" and then walk away when I assure them that I'm very excited indeed, and that if I'm eating Toblerone chocolate, it's only to disguise the tension. The sole person who remains aboard the train is a Russian with a grim expression, perhaps a diplomat serving in Finland, who occupies at the same time both compartments two and five. This man's son keeps going back and forth between the two compartments, saying "excuse me" to everyone in English, and generally making everyone hate him. He's a chubby eleven-year-old, the Soviet version of a little American raised on cheeseburgers and milkshakes: a Boston Celtics T-shirt, jeans, and track shoes. The Vermont retirees look at him and seem happy: children, the wife tells the husband, really are the same everywhere around the world.

The train pulls out and arrives in Luzhaika, a Soviet border crossing. Two policemen board the train and ask the passengers to stand up, to make sure that there's no one hiding in the space below the mattresses, as if they were afraid of a possible invasion by an army of contortionists. The Soviet Union that stretches out before the Repin Express seems like a country that's just emerged from a time machine: old cars, motorcycles with sidecars, elderly female level-crossing guards with pitiless gazes, like Socialist women always have when they're given a badge, a cap, or an official paddle. Before Vyborg (which was Finnish until 1940, and used to be called Viipuri), the railway runs among and over the little lakes that fringe the Gulf of Finland. This section of the journey is a symphony of undergarments: fishermen in their underpants, soldiers in sleeveless undershirts, and two young girls working a pedal boat, bare legs flying. Only after the passage of the tenth railcar do they notice that an entire trainful of people knows what color their panties are, and they cover their eyes, laughing.

At Vyborg, I'm informed by the *Thomas Cook European Rail Timetable,* the train ought to stop for twenty-five minutes. Just to be sure, Ortensia pulls out her Russian phrase book. *"Skolka vryeminy budyit stoyat poyezd?"* she asks. How long will the train be stopping here?

"Twenty-five minutes," the conductor replies in English, as he hangs on the windows to make sure they really are closed, per regulation. Of course, that isn't true. When the Repin Express pulls out again ten minutes later, heading for Leningrad, I'm a member of the small crowd chasing after it and cursing.

As the train continues through the woods, the little boy keeps walking back and forth in the corridor, "excuse me" resonating with murderous regularity. The father, realizing that his son is becoming unpopular, drags him off to the dining car, where I'll soon be forced to join them. The menu is lavish, but as is so often the case in these parts, it's nothing but a list of good intentions, or perhaps a tombstone commemorating all the exquisite dishes that have been consumed on these tables over the years. This evening the selection is soup, bread and cheese, and cucumbers. No beer, just water that reeks of sulfur. No wine, but a crate of empty bottles of Soviet spumante sold who knows when and to who knows whom. The waiter smiles only when he writes up the check, probably because he's embarrassed to ask twenty-five Finnish markkas for three rubles and fifty-seven kopecks. To prove that his accounting is accurate, he reaches into his pocket and pulls out a musical calculator: each digit is a different note; after the addition sign, two notes; after the equal sign, a short melody. I pay the twenty-five Finnish markkas; it's too much for bread and cheese, but the concert is certainly worth it.

While the retirees from Vermont are busy trying to find the station of Zelenogorsk on a world map, and the Soviet boy bombards even the Russian waiter with "excuse me's," the train runs past wooden houses and birch trees, passes Repino, and arrives in Leningrad, at the Finland Station, in the intense light of the northern evening. The station, which is said to be quite lovely, was built to plans by the architects Ashastin, Baranov, and Lukin between 1955 and 1960. In front of it is a statue of Lenin, who on April 16, 1917, arrived at this station, after ten years of exile and seven days of travel in another train—that one, too, with its windows shut, but probably with a better dining car. Those were different times: Lenin found the Bolsheviks of Saint Petersburg waiting to welcome him, and he harangued them from the turret of an armored car. I have to settle for a taxi driver who heads off toward the Pribaltiyskaya Hotel, though it's actually in the opposite direction, but it's not a serious mistake: the longer the drive, the more time he has to try to sell me watches, caviar, stacks of rubles, and a T-shirt with the slogan "Lenin Rocks," which he pulls out of the glove compartment. Vladimir Ilyich Ulyanov could have worn it, if he'd had a sense of humor, while marching toward the Winter Palace.

White Nights on the Leningrad Ekspress

According to Intourist in Leningrad, a person with any common sense has no reason to go all the way to Warsaw by train. If you absolutely must go to Warsaw, take a plane. If you insist on taking a train, then you're not a person with a shred of common sense. These rigid convictions are reflected in the train reservations, which appear and disappear like rabbits in a magician's top hat: two days before the trip, there's room on the Leningrad Ekspress; one day before departure, the seat has vanished; four hours before departure, the seat reappears. All I need to do is rush over to the Varshavsky Voksal, the Warsaw Station, in car no. 8513, at the courteous expense of Intourist itself, with a driver who either is in a bad mood or else wants a tip.

Standing guard at the station is the usual statue of Lenin scanning the horizon, the work of the sculptor N. Tomsky, who, along with his colleagues S. Evseev, M. Kharlamov, V. Kozlov, A. Kriyanovskaya, and M. Anikushin, filled Leningrad with "monuments to the leaders of the proletariat, founders of scientific Communism." As so often happens in Russian stations, in order to reach the trains, you don't enter the building; you go around it, making your way through the usual crowds loaded down with packages. There are many Poles who have come to Leningrad to buy appliances and sell them back home. A man, a woman, and a child go by, transporting a refrigerator of truly daunting size. They will wrestle it into the compartment next to mine, and they'll travel with it for twenty-four hours, like a family transporting their loved one's corpse.

The Leningrad Ekspress departs right on time, at 4:10 p.m., and rolls silently through the outskirts of town, where everyone's busy celebrating the short summer season. Ahead of it stretches 718 miles of track: heading southwest, it will run through the Pskov Oblast (Pskov Region) for the whole afternoon; it will enter Latvia around midnight; three hours later it will be in Lithuania, the land that in the 1930s changed hands between Russian and German overlords; at dawn it will reach Belarus; and it will be on the Polish plains around noon. We'll eventually arrive in Warsaw in midafternoon.

The journey promises to be long, therefore, and this is good news. For twenty-four hours we'll have nothing to worry about. In Communist Eastern Europe the problem with trains is boarding them; once you're aboard, however, you don't have anything else to worry about until the next train and the next fight to buy a ticket and get on board. The compartment is cozy, and no smaller than a Soviet hotel room; the walls are lined with plastic that looks like wood, while the table is made of wood that looks like plastic. The beds are comfortable and the neighbors are silent. When we lower the window for ventilation, it won't stay down, but a small piece of engineering solves the problem: we hang one of our travel bags off the handle, and the Russian air then has free access. Robert Louis Stevenson was right when he described the attractions of railway trains in these words: "The train disturbs so little the scenes through which it takes us, that our heart becomes full of the placidity and stillness of the country; and while the body is borne forward in the flying chain of carriages, the thoughts alight, as the humour moves them, at unfrequented stations. . . ." In other words, it's nice to travel in a self-propelled bedroom, with a documentary streaming past outside the window.

Truth be told, there are a few snafus, but nothing much to speak of. A conductor speaks to me in Russian for ten minutes, and when I tell him, "I'm not Russian," he replies with a grin, "Neither am I; I'm Estonian." There are no tables available in the dining car; it is garrisoned by young Polish couples who silently gulp down chicken and lemonade, the only items on the menu. Last of all, there is Vladimir, the *konduktor* who's in charge of our carriage: he insists that the customs form exists only in Russian and in Polish, so we're just going to have to deal with that.

The Leningrad Ekspress runs across black peaty earth, flax fields, and bogs. Around sunset, it stops without warning in several microscopic stations, where no one gets off and no one gets on. These stops, however, meet with the approval of the local population: whole families, with little kids and picnic baskets, have come out to see the train, and sitting on the grassy banks, they entertain the passengers while we entertain them. At Strugi Krasnye a husband and wife shout out that it's *beautiful* to see an *italianski* head poke out of a train window on an August evening. At Novoselye the audience consists of young couples who all look the same pushing baby carriages: he's wearing track shoes and linen pants, while her T-shirt is too tight and her hair is pulled back in a bun.

After Pskov, which has a station painted aquamarine, the same color as the churches of Leningrad, we see cranes perched on one leg, poised atop light poles. After Ostrov, where the station is a candy pink, Vladimir the conductor appears, apparently tipsy and carrying three blankets, three quilts, three sets of sheets, three pillows, three pillowcases, and six towels, almost as if he were hoping to make up for the shortage of dishes on the menu with this gesture of abundance. We arrive in Rēzekne after midnight; we're in Latvia now and Vladimir reappears, well and truly drunk, shouting: "*Idite za mnoy!* [Come with me!] I've found the party." Incredibly, it's true.

The party, as he calls it, is three cars away, in a compartment where four Russians are traveling with an unspecified quantity of cans of caviar, watches, Paul McCartney record albums in Soviet editions, chocolates, salamis, and Pepsodent toothpaste. Three men and a woman: one man says his name is Valentin, another is Nikolai, the young woman is named Violeta, and the fourth member of the party says nothing but drinks Georgian cognac as if it were orangeade. They tell me that they're assiduous clients of the Leningrad Ekspress: for business, not for pleasure. In Warsaw, Valentin explains, people have nothing, and so they buy everything; unfortunately, they pay in zlotys, a currency that is virtually worthless. I ask him whether he's tired of living on a train. He replies: "It's better than living on a ship, which is what I did until last year. Do you know that I was the executive officer aboard a freighter, and I earned one-fiftieth of what a cabin boy on an American ship makes, simply because he is paid in dollars?"

Nikolai pours more cognac and tells of a smuggler's hard life. "The Poles don't like us Russians," he says, "but who cares? Caviar, if you want it, is five dollars, and Soviet Paul McCartney records are ten dollars: in America, collectors will pay two hundred dollars for them. If you invite me to Italy, you'd be doing me a favor; if you invite me in the name of Greenpeace, so much the better. I like Gorbachev, but he doesn't understand us smugglers."

Valentin listens, cuts salami, and hums. The conductor Vladimir repeats for the fifth time that he has customs forms only in Russian and in Polish, and that it's my problem if I know neither Russian nor Polish. The blond Violeta, with the eyeglasses and makeup of a 1950s high school girl, says nothing, smokes Moskva cigarettes, and looks at her reflection in the windows until it's five in the morning, when the neon lights of the city of Vilnius appear and the Lithuanians, in the darkness, begin their peaceful assault on the Leningrad Ekspress. "Are you Russian?" I ask two female students. "Not on your life," the younger one replies. "We're Lithuanians."

In Grodno—which has changed hands over the centuries between Tartars, Lithuanians, Poles, and Russians—it is the Russians who check our passports. In Kuźnica Białostocka the train cars are hoisted into the air to put on narrower axles, suitable to the European gauge. As the train runs across the plains, the Poles start pushing their refrigerator toward the exits, cursing because the corridors are so narrow. In uniform and slippers, conductor Vladimir battles against his headache. Violeta continues looking, with decided disinterest, at the world outside her glasses and the train window. Nikolai talks about a Polish friend who spends his life in trains, from Warsaw to Beijing. In every station along the Trans-Siberian Express, he sells something. With the money he earns along the way, he purchases a monkey in China, takes it back to Poland, and sells it for many dollars to university laboratories. If I'm interested in a monkey, I should just let him know.

5:55 a.m.: Ekspresowy Berolina

The train stations of Eastern Europe should be toured at dawn, when people are walking around briskly, and before they acquire the defeated expression that comes with the first humiliations of the day. Even Warsaw's Central Station, at that time of the morning, is almost pretty: a reassuring mastodon, a monument to the Polskie Koleje Państwowe, the Polish railways, a place where only the Poles, apparently, can find their way around. For everyone else, it's a labyrinth, and the signs aren't signs: they're sleight-of-hand tricks performed with consonants. This is how an American guidebook describes it: "Warszawa Centralna consists of four levels. On the first level are arrivals (*przyjazdy*) and departures (*odjazdy*). On the second floor are the connections with buses and taxis. On the third level, you can purchase tickets for the departures of the day. The ticket windows from 1 to 11 are also for making reservations for certain specific destinations; the windows from 12 to 16 are for reservations for any destination at all. If you are in line for windows 1 to 11, check to see the destination written above the window. If it's not listed, you're in the wrong line. Write on a sheet of paper the time of your train, your destination, and the desired class, and show it to the ticket clerk. On the fourth level, you can buy tickets for trips within the next two months." Perhaps you can understand why the guidebook concludes: "Don't go to the Warsaw train station to buy tickets, go to a tourism office."

With tickets in hand, however, it's not impossible to find your train. The Ekspresowy Berolina, the express train to East Berlin, departs daily at 5:55 a.m., and anyone will be able to point you to the right *peron* (platform). The train arrives from the Warszawa Wschodnia station, which is on the other side of the Vistula River, and it stops for exactly thirteen minutes. When the train departs, my compartment offers a representative assortment of Poles: a young engineer who alternates reading the poetry of Czeslaw Milosz and a copy of *Trybuna Ludu*, the newspaper of the Polish United Workers' Party; a blond matron who reads nothing and simply smiles full-time; a teacher, with the kind of mustache and blow-dried hair that you only ever really see in the photographs posted on hairdressers' windows; and last of all an oversized young man in his early twenties who yawns, hiccups, noisily digests, takes off his running shoes, and checks to see what's inside them. When he gets off at Kutno, after two hours on the train, we survivors all exchange relieved glances.

Until we reach Poznan, which is midway between Warsaw and Berlin, there's room in the compartment only for a maelstrom of rote courtesies in many languages: the Poles, among themselves, in Polish; the schoolteacher, with me, in French; the engineer, in English. A couple of peasants, who boarded at Kutno and are heading for Świebodzin, explain to everyone in German that it was the conductor who sent them to first class with a second-class ticket, because their car—no. 36—was nowhere to be found. For the rest of the trip, they'll sit with their eyes on the door and their tickets in hand, expecting an announcement that car no. 36 has finally been found, and that their ride in first class has therefore come to an end.

These are momentous days for Poland, a country that is certainly used to momentous days. Solidarity is asking to form a government; General Jaruzelski has been made president; Prime Minister Rakowski has succeeded him as party leader. The market for agricultural products has just been liberalized, consumer prices in certain instances have jumped fivefold, and people fear riots in the streets. There's every reason for the passengers on the Ekspresowy Berolina to be eager to express their opinions, which is something Poles are always willing to do. Along with the Russians and the Israelis, in fact, they're the world's most politically loquacious people. For years, prudence has suggested the wisdom of restraining that impulse, but now they can almost taste freedom, and they're giving the impression they want to make up for lost time.

After Poznan, the engineer looks around, and starts unburdening himself in English. "What do you think of Poland?" he begins. I tell him: "It's a friendly, fascinating country, with an inept government clinging to an anachronistic ideology. But you'll get by." He smiles, unconvinced, and then he explains why his country is on the brink of collapse. "I have a university degree, I'm thirty-seven, and I have a wife and two children. I'm a state employee, and I earn sixty thousand zlotys a month. Since a dollar is worth six thousand zlotys, I earn ten dollars a month, right? If I came to Italy to work as a field hand—remember, I'm an engineer—I'd earn at least five hundred dollars a month. In other words, I'd earn fifty times as much, right? That's why the young people want to leave, my dear friend. Because we're the beggars of Europe, and the latest appointments make me laugh: the party leader who becomes president, the prime minister who becomes party leader, the minister of the interior who wants to become prime minister. It's always the same people, and they aren't even slightly ashamed. Right? No, it's not right!" At this point he falls silent. The peasants of Świebodzin look at him happily. Since the engineer was speaking in English, they didn't understand a thing, but they're in first class.

The Ekspresowy Berolina approaches the Oder River, rolling across the plain through the region named Wielkopolska, "greater Poland," a land that had the misfortune of finding itself in the wrong corner of Europe and has paid the price: there's no counting the invasions and battles that have taken place in these fields. In the corridor, a young blond woman in a tracksuit has arrived and is looking out at the flat countryside outside the window. She has eyes and a figure that on an Italian train would guarantee that she'd be left alone for thirty seconds at the most. She's a twenty-one-year-old born in Poznan named Agnieszka. She works in an Italian restaurant in West Berlin, and she detests her compatriots. "They're too poor," she says. "I'm ashamed of them." She detests this Polish train, the Polish conductors, and the Polish customs officers. She detests the West Germans, "because they despise us Poles and all they drink at the restaurant is prosecco." She detests the East German conductors, who are constantly on the hunt for *Ausreisewillige*, "those who want to leave" for the West without permission. Agnieszka asks whether there are Poles in Italy. I tell her that there are. "And what do they do? Horrible things, I can imagine. Don't even tell me. I detest the Poles in Italy."

The train arrives in Frankfurt an der Oder, the first city in the German Democratic Republic, surrounded on both sides by streamers that read: "Welcome, Young Pioneers!" The conductor explains that in order to continue on to West Berlin, we will need to move from the fourth carriage, where we now are, to the first carriage, because the rest of the train will be decoupled at the Hauptbahnhof of East Berlin. As we drag our luggage down the crowded corridors, customs agents and policemen decide to start checking passengers again. First they stamp passports; then they take our currency declarations; last of all, they inspect the baggage. Each time we are obliged to open bags and suitcases, to the mockery of the Germans packed into the corridors. The last conductor is a little man with a big, sad, droopy mustache, and he asks Agnieszka something in Polish. She turns sharply around and hisses a single word. He opens his eyes, turns red, and flees. "He wanted to know what I had in my bag," Agnieszka explains with a big smile. "*Panties*, I told him."

While we speak, the train enters the eastern outskirts of Berlin. We've run out of time; there's no way we're going to make it to the first carriage before the train stops. Oh well, the passengers heading for the West will just hop off at the station and move up the platform to the first carriage, right? Alas, as we'll discover, once you get off, it's forbidden to reboard. We're now going to have to take the subway and S-Bahn to the Friedrichstraße station, get in line, and cross the border on foot, dragging our suitcases after us. The passport and luggage checks are very slow: more than two hours, half of that in the rain. First Agnieszka laughs; then she curses; then she falls silent. She has a Polish passport and the Berlin Wall to get through. You can't be born in Poznan and— when faced with the eyes of a policeman, a passport stamp, and a border—fail to feel small and be a little afraid.

Fasting on the Istanbul Express

When the Orient Express, on October 4, 1883, left Paris on its inaugural trip, it took several journalists along, an indication that the profession even then had instincts for everything that's luxurious and free of charge. They described, with an abundance of details, the delights of the train that connected two worlds, Europe and Asia. The bathrooms were lined with Italian marble, the lounge car was furnished like a London club, the glasses were made of Baccarat crystal, and the appetizers were based on oysters and caviar. A few minor details have changed, let us say: on the Istanbul Express there is no first-class service, there is no dining car, and the marble bathrooms have been replaced by an explanation (fifty-four separate points) in Bulgarian concerning the operation of the restrooms. There are, however, hundreds of Turks, who toss bags of garbage out the window, which, perhaps because they seem unable to hit anyone, they keep on trying for the rest of the trip.

Before boarding the Istanbul Express, I had taken a train at dawn from Berlin south through the German Democratic Republic, running past the giant factories dedicated to Walter Ulbricht, through cities with names as hard as rock (Lutherstadt Wittenberg), leaving the great northern European plain near Leipzig, rising through the mountains, and entering the Federal Republic of Germany. Toward evening, the Istanbul Express, a Yugoslavian and Bulgarian train, departs Munich. The Serbian conductor cooks onions and pork in his lodgings and wants to be left alone, the Turkish emigrants are busy with their farewells, and lanky Scandinavian couples are sharing bread and chocolate, each eyeing with greater fondness the chocolate in the hands of his or her traveling companion. This hardly seems like the train of Graham Greene and Agatha Christie, nor the one in which Lady Diana, Maurice Dekobra's heroine (in *The Madonna of the Sleeping Cars*, 1925), announced: "I have a ticket for Constantinople. But I may stop off at Vienna or Budapest. That depends absolutely on chance or the color of the eyes of my neighbor in the compartment."

This express to the Orient arrives at the Yugoslavian border around midnight, and the Slovenian customs officers throw open the doors to the compartments with all the courtesy of John Wayne barging into a saloon. Following them comes the Serbian conductor, breath reeking of onions as he announces, "Croatians, Slovenians, and Serbs all get along," and ten minutes later, he sticks his head back in and says, "That's not true." Last of all comes a policeman, who starts out with these words: "You foreigners are crazy to ride on our trains, with our tracks that are one jolt after another, and the danger of getting your passports stolen." I thank him for the heartfelt encouragement and try to get some sleep, trying to make up my mind whether it's *papirni ubrusi* that means "paper towels" in Serbo-Croatian, while *zabranjeno pušenje* means "no smoking," or whether it's the other way around.

After an agitated night, during the course of which Slovenians, Croatians, and Serbs take turns shouting outside the train windows in various stations, the Istanbul Express arrives in Belgrade, where several cars disappear. I'm moved to a Bulgarian second-class berth, which is better than the American humorist Robert Benchley might have led one to expect in the 1930s ("Traveling with children corresponds roughly to traveling third class in Bulgaria"). The cars are reasonably clean, and the conductor—who has the contented demeanor of a delicatessen butcher—offers me a bottle of Balgarsko Pivo, the beer of the Balkans, and makes sure to walk close to Scandinavian girls in tunnels, hoping for a sudden jolt of the train.

Niš, in southern Serbia, constituted the last outpost until 1889 for those who rode in the cars of the Orient Express. Here passengers were loaded onto stagecoaches and transported to the Bulgarian city of Tatar Pazardzhik (little market of the Tatars), 175 miles away, a trip that the Compagnie Internationale des Wagons-Lits did its very best to present as a captivating adventure, but which actually unfolded under the greedy eyes of Turkish, Serbian, Bulgarian, and Macedonian bandits. A hundred years later, the great-grandsons of those same bandits wave at the train as they fish on the river Nišava, surround it in the Palanka railway station, and spy on it at Pirot, the ancient Roman Turres—famous for its carpets and for a hotel, Le Roi de Serbie, where at the end of the nineteenth century an overnight stay cost a single Belgian franc. Any room they assigned you was always "the king's room," in commemoration of some passing king, never accurately identified.

Once we pass through Tsaribrod—nowadays called Dimitrovgrad, in honor of the Bulgarian Lenin—the train enters Bulgaria and seems to take on the indolent ways of the Balkans: it stops for no reason by a stand of fruit trees, half-built houses, and local trains (*putnichki*), which seem to have been left there to fill up the landscape, but instead suddenly depart, with their load of wide-eyed women and children, heading off toward some tiny destination with a name written in Cyrillic characters. Around here, back in the day, King Boris of Bulgaria would stop the Orient Express and, claiming that the railways were his own personal property, take the controls of the locomotive and indulge his love of trains. Obsessed with a fear of delays, he'd always drive at top speed, endangering the boilers and the coronary arteries of engineers and firemen, who would turn pale whenever they saw him coming down the tracks in his white uniform. The Compagnie Internationale des Wagons-Lits, which was afraid of making a royal enemy, never did figure out how to discourage him.

We arrive in Sofia while the sun shines low under the cantilevered platform roofs, and armed soldiers keep passengers from approaching the train. The Turkish guest workers of Nuremberg and Berlin shoot anxious glances out the window, and for an hour they abstain from throwing trash onto the tracks. As the train departs for Plovdiv and we plunge into our second night, the sensation begins to spread among the passengers of now being residents of the Istanbul Express: they stroll; they converse; they stretch their sheets over their bunks and watch the sun sink behind the Vakarel Pass, where Frederick Barbarossa's crusaders once marched, full of intentions both holy and wicked. In Kostenets the railway crosses the Maritsa River, and then descends into the plains. It leaves behind it the lights of Pazardzhik, which in 1870 still had twenty mosques and was the third-largest market in the Turkish Empire; it stops for ten minutes in Plovdiv, the Philippopolis of Philip of Macedon, father of Alexander the Great; it continues rolling toward the border, running past empty streets, forsaken outskirts, tobacco fields, and a brightly lit discotheque, which glitters for a moment in the darkness and then vanishes again in the night of eastern Thracia.

In Svilengrad, Bulgarian policemen wake everyone up just before two in the morning, banging their flashlights like clubs on the doors of the compartments. At four in the morning, it's their Turkish counterparts' turn; they force the passengers to get off at Kapikule and line up in front of a station office. The train doesn't depart until six thirty in the morning, leaving behind it the mountains of household possessions of the Bulgarians who are fleeing their faltering country; it passes Edirne, the ancient Adrianople, and runs through fields of sunflowers and dust. It rolls past Cerkezköv, where in 1891 a group of rebels under the orders of a certain Anasthatos derailed the Orient Express and took twenty prisoners. Only around noon does it heave within view of the Sea of Marmara. The train, running two hours late, pulls into Istanbul's Sirkeci Terminal, which is separated from Helsinki by 3,114 miles of Actually Existing Socialism.

I didn't know at the time that I'd witnessed, from a train, the last summer of Communism. And after the summer comes the fall. In the following months Soviet-backed regimes in Poland, East Germany, Czechoslovakia, Hungary, Romania, and Bulgaria collapsed. The Soviet Union (USSR) itself dissolved at the end of 1991.

9

From Naples to London:
Across Europe with Little Donald

Shaking his head, Donald Trump approaches Stazione Napoli Centrale on Wednesday afternoon. When people see him, they smile. He ignores everyone, from the lowly vantage point of his pedestal. He hasn't purchased a ticket, but that's no cause for concern: bobbleheads travel free. *"Chillo è pazz', e o' coreano chiatto è pure peggio!"* hisses a matron in Neapolitan dialect as she passes us. "That guy's crazy, and the fat Korean is even worse." She doesn't like Kim Jong-un, of course. She has no idea that I'm going to have to travel with the other character for the entire three-day duration of the train trip that lies ahead of me.

I'm taking a train from Naples all the way to London. I want to know what Europeans think of Donald Trump, a year after his election. Why the bobblehead statuette? Well, first things first: unlike the original, it keeps its mouth shut and it doesn't tweet. More than that, my traveling companion has a singular advantage. I won't have to ask strangers what they think of Donald Trump. They'll approach and tell me, unasked. (*Wrong!* as Mr. Trump would say.)

The 3:15 train to Rome and Milan awaits us at Track 8. It's not easy to get there. Our photographer, Giulio Piscitelli, is forced to lie on the pavement, Trump-high. This doesn't go unnoticed. A crowd starts to form. One distinguished-looking Neapolitan professional, with his standard-issue briefcase, chuckles: "As long as he stays small, I'm okay with it. But what if he gets a swelled head and decides to run for the White House?"

Two illegal vendors (selling socks, for the most part) come over. One of them has a sky-blue T-shirt with an English-language slogan: "Camels can go two weeks without drinking. I can't." From his breath, I'd have to say he means what his T-shirt says. The other vendor, who wears a baseball cap, asks if he can take a selfie with mini-Trump. He read one of my books about America, years ago. He quotes from it, accurately, and says: "Back in your day, there was no Trump, was there?" Then he heads straight for a gang of tourists.

Naples–Rome–Milan

The train pulls out on schedule: mini-Trump begins his trip across Europe. I place him on the tray table in front of me, in the recessed holder meant for a beverage: he fits perfectly. The little statuette wins an unspoken popularity contest. People go by, see him, and generally smile. Are they smiling because they are silent Trump supporters or because they think the bobblehead is funny? Or maybe *I* am funny? I'll never know. I can't question every smile on the railway. Occasionally, a passerby will shoot me a worried glance: someone who goes around with Trump, the glance suggests, might be capable of anything.

The conductor comes through checking tickets. "He rides free," he informs me seriously, gazing at mini-Trump. Two teenagers look up from their cell phones and say: "Trump was voted in by the middle class as a thumb in the eye to the elites." Signor Tommaso Mestria, who works for the postal service, stops and opines: "The bobblehead is cute; Trump himself, not so much. In any case, he's not going to be

impeached. He's going to serve the next three years in the White
House. No doubt about it, Americans are weird." Then he changes the
subject to Italian politics.

The train stops at Rome's Termini station, and then pulls out again.
Little Trump watches as the train races north through Italy and the
afternoon descends into evening. I change my seat, to avoid the low
afternoon sunlight, but in Bologna four young women board the train
and, rightly, claim their ticketed seats. I ask them if they want to keep
Trump until Milan. "Thanks, but let's not and say we did," they reply.

Little Trump, in the silent high-speed train car, is a star. I suspect
some passengers pretend to need the lavatory so they can come close
and look at him. Some make faces; one snorts; a few roll their eyes.
References to Silvio Berlusconi? None. That may come as a surprise to
my American readers, but I expected it. True, the similarities between
the two men are obvious. Both are loud, vain, blustering businessmen,
amateur politicians, and professional womanizers. Both have a troubled relationship with their egos and their hair. Both think God is their
publicist, and twist religion to suit their own ends. There is a difference,
though. Mr. Berlusconi was the longest-serving Italian head of government since World War II (not much came out of it, apart from a lasting
friendship with Vladimir Putin); but today, in a troubled world, he's
seen by many Italians as an avuncular, reassuring figure. Mr. Trump,
the demagogue in chief, is still controversial—everywhere, even in the
bobblehead version on a high-speed Italian train.

Half an hour out of Milan, a well-dressed young woman sitting a
couple of yards away points to the statuette. "The company that makes
that thing is called Royal Bobbles, and is headquartered in Alpharetta,
Georgia." Excuse me, but how do you happen to know that? "The work
I do." Do you work for Trump? "No, no. But those little bobblehead
statues generate issues that you couldn't begin to imagine. I work in the
field of intellectual property, trademarks, copyright, you know? I'm on
my way from Rome now—that's exactly what I've just been working

on." Wait, there's an Italian who's being considered for bobblehead status? Who? I ask in astonishment. "That I can't tell you. You'd never guess the name, and anyway, whoever said it was an Italian?" she replies with a smile. I take her business card: her name is Silvia and she works for a well-known international law firm in Milan. I'm left with my curiosity unslaked. Trump, as always, remains impassive: he's not interested in knowing who his successors will be.

Milan–Paris

The next morning, another train, this time to Paris. The TGV leaves from Porta Garibaldi station at 8:45. Trump is sticking out of my backpack, with his usual spiteful glare. Two boys stop me: "Excuse me, sir, why is he in your backpack?"

"I'm taking him to London."

They exchange a glance, and then, as if my answer made perfect sense, reply: "Oh, of course." On the train, the air-conditioning is icy—most unusual, in Europe—and the silence is surreal. It seems this train knows it's about to leave talkative Italy and entering more introverted France.

Turin's Porta Susa station in the sunlight, then Oulx Sestriere, followed by Bardonecchia and the border. The first French city is Modane. France tumbles down out of the mountains. The train speeds along over the plains and alongside lakes. We leave Lyon to the west. The light of continental Europe bounces off the water and into the sky. The Donald—credit where credit is due—proves to be an excellent traveling companion. He lets me read, never budges from his recessed cup holder, and silently listens to the hushed rustling of newspapers. Maybe he's waiting for me to finish the article in *The Economist* that talks about him.

////////////////

In this car, talking on the phone is forbidden, but some of us don't seem to know that. Thus, all of these are duly scolded: yours truly, who in turn scolds an Englishman, who thereupon scolds a German. All my attempts to introduce the forty-fifth American president into the conversation fail miserably. If my fellow passengers are not allowed to speak on the phone, fair enough, they won't. But they don't want to talk about Donald Trump?

The statuette, as we have seen, belongs to the bobblehead series. These characters are also known as Nodders (because of the way their heads nod) or Wobblers (ditto). Basically, when they are moved, they shake their heads. And on a train, that means their heads never stand still. Those who pass by and happen to spot The Donald where you might expect a bottle of mineral water shake their heads, too. "Do you mind my telling you that that thing gets on my nerves?" says a woman with a Piedmontese accent. Just like the original does, I tell her.

The company, as we've learned, is based in Alpharetta, Georgia. I visited there in 2009, at the height of the subprime crisis. It would never have occurred to me that I might one day travel with what might fairly be considered an honorary citizen. Bobblehead statues have different prices. The most expensive are the customized versions: for $79 you can have your mother-in-law's head (on a premade body); for $145, you can get your whole mother-in-law from the circles under her eyes to her big toes. On the Web site www.bobbleheads.com, The (mass-produced) Donald costs only $19.95. As I look at him, I feel a twinge of pity. So cheap.

After traveling through the Morvan Regional Natural Park, I strike up a conversation with Gianni, a retired cardiologist, former member of Lotta Continua, a militant left-wing organization, and an impassioned partisan of the creation of a united Kurdistan (revolutionaries always seem to find a revolution!). He goes to Paris frequently, and is full of youthful enthusiasm. He has an opinion about Trump: "These days, the left turns up its nose at the neglected corners of society. When I was young, we were always out in the working-class quarters and on the street. We understood the fears and the dreams of ordinary people. That no longer happens. The left—in Italy, in Europe, in the U.S.—is only interested in national party politics. They don't work on the ground anymore! That opens up the market for the populists and their simplistic message. They convince voters that, hey, their savior is around the corner! That's how people like Trump get elected."

And so? "And so the blue-collar worker has a tactical vision. The intellectual ought to have a more strategic vision." I actually don't quite understand what he means, but I feel like I've gone back to the vibrant discussions at the political rallies I attended in high school, and I don't mind the sensation.

In Paris

We pull into Paris, Gare de Lyon.

The photographer waiting for me at the station, Michel Setboun, is a celebrity. He documented the Iranian revolution in 1979, publishing his photographs in many leading American publications. He still goes back to Tehran frequently, where he published a monumental book. As a result, he is no longer allowed to set foot in the United States. Which makes him angry. "I was in New York on 9/11. I have photographs in the Ground Zero museum! And I'm not allowed to go back to America. Because I've been to Iran. Does that make sense to you?"

That said, Michel takes The Donald and carries him around the Gare de Lyon, positioning him here and there. He's not sure he's going to be able to take pictures. He's afraid he'll be stopped by the police. "Well, I just took a picture of that woman in a burqa, a garment that is forbidden in France. So if they try to stop me, I'll tell them: 'Wait, her yes, and Trump no?'" The logic eludes me, but Setboun is so kind and likable that we agree to meet for a beer in a Marais bistro, Au Petit Fer à Cheval. There, too, mini-Trump, standing on the counter, is immensely popular. But in Paris the man himself is not well liked; in fact, no one offers to buy him a drink. Only one woman, a smiling American of Irish descent, puts in a good word for him. She is blond and petite. From the height of her barstool, she offers me a glossy black and gold business card. Maureen Donovan, an immigration lawyer, has this to say, with a sigh: "Trump makes me angry, but he does create plenty of paying work for me."

Paris—London

The next morning, the Eurostar pulls out of the Gare du Nord at 10:13. Lots of security, not many people, airport atmosphere. But the train doesn't take off into the sky; instead it leaves Paris, heads north, descends under the waters of the Channel, and heads to London. Mini-Trump returns to his post on the tray table. The attendant—Jean-Christophe, according to his name tag—offers mini-Trump a cup of coffee, utterly deadpan. But he does it in French, so mini-Trump ignores him, the same as he did the rest of Europe.

Eight armed border policemen are traveling aboard the train: they're relieving their fellow officers at our destination, in London. The French border controls are in the UK; the British border controls are in France—at point of departure on either end of the line. So passengers can just walk out of the station on arrival in both Paris and London (and illegal migrants are not allowed to board the train in the first place). One of the policemen comes over, leans on the table, and studies mini-Trump wordlessly. "Don't arrest him," I say. He smiles and introduces himself: his name is Claude; he's going to retire soon. He has a weather-beaten face from an American Western. "The things we've seen, lately, with illegal immigrants. By now, I can spot a fake ID just by sense of touch. The real problem is that some of them have real IDs but fake identities. Those come in all day Saturday and Sunday. They know that the prefectures are closed and we have no way of checking. All we have here is one train and one tunnel. And he"—pointing at Trump—"wants to build a wall along the Mexican border? How many miles long is that? Almost two thousand? Just makes me laugh."

We emerge from the Channel tunnel and slide into the English light. Soon we're in London. St. Pancras station welcomes us with its red bricks. Little Trump, who's riding in the breast pocket of my jacket, immediately becomes a star. A British woman who's just left the train comes over to give him a kiss. Wojcek, a young man from Danzig who's just arrived in England, asks for a selfie. A group of Japanese tourists laughs enthusiastically. I leave the station and catch a black cab to the Reform Club. The cabbie is named Jeremy. He spots mini-Trump sticking out of my backpack. "A few days ago one of my fares was Kazuo Ishiguro, who just received the Nobel Prize in Literature. And today I have Donald Trump. This is definitely my week!" We pull up on Pall Mall and he offers me a special discount.

I invite an American friend to lunch at the Reform Club—Anne Applebaum, Pulitzer Prize–winning columnist for the *Washington Post*. Her husband comes with her: Radek Sikorski, longtime Polish minister of foreign affairs, now highly critical toward the direction politics is taking in Warsaw. We've all known one another since 1989. We talk about the American presidential election of 2016, and how the Russians made use of Facebook and Twitter to support Donald Trump (Anne wrote about this early on, and at the time many didn't believe her). The subject of our conversation, in handy travel format, was left in the front lobby of the Reform Club. The lobby in which, according to *Around the World in Eighty Days*, Phileas Fogg made his celebrated wager.

No doubt about it, Jules Verne had a wild imagination. But not even he could have dreamed up The Donald.

10

What to Bring

What a beautiful respite a train journey is
and a good book, too, and best of all the book on the train,
in life and out of it at the same time.

TIM PARKS, *ITALIAN WAYS*

Maps

It dawns on me that I've taken the wrong train, but it's already pulled out of the station. I ask directions: "Excuse me, where are we going?" People answer me (a few courteously, others reluctantly). I realize that I don't know any of the destinations they mention to me. Not one.

"This is a train for Vigliante. It will arrive this evening."

"Where does it stop?"

"Roccaglia, Arbule, Casamagna."

"Can you tell me the name of a bigger city?"

"Sperantia, we'll be there in an hour."

Out the wet train window, I see a city drawing closer. The tracks begin to proliferate; lighted windows pierce the mist. I think, *Those people know where they live, but I don't know where I am.* The usual station sign appears, white letters on a blue background. SPERANTIA. A town I've never heard of. I get out of the train; I read the departure board: there must be a regional train heading to some familiar place. Tiny orange letters indicate unknown localities: Evalanche, Turilo, Sargenta.

I walk out onto the piazza in front of the station; there are trolleys headed to New Sperantia, West Lucido, Asmaro.

I go back in, anxiously, and board another train, packed with commuters who are all busy with their cell phones. Sooner or later this train will reach a city I know, I think to myself. Or a city that I don't know, but which has connections to a city I do. I'm uneasy, but I can't say so. It's as if someone had changed the world.

Luckily, I wake up.

This is what I dreamed, while I was finishing the first draft of this book. Maybe I'm thinking and writing too much about trains. And so the trains decided to take my dreams, as well.

But they did it courteously, reminding me of an important fact: trains move on the terrain of human beings, and that terrain should never be taken for granted. You need to respect it. And in order to respect it, you need to know it.

Certainly, some travelers overdo it. They travel not in the world but inside a map, a tour guide, or an app. TripAdvisor doesn't recommend; it commands you. Expedia limits experimentation. Life outside, to many, must match what's written inside. If that doesn't happen, they find it disquieting.

This is hardly a new phenomenon. I remember, thirty years ago on the Trans-Siberian Express, people who knew every station, who anticipated every railway switch, who interpreted every horizon. Useful traveling companions, provided you don't spend too much time with them. They couldn't see Europe as it turned into Asia, the eyes and the colors as they changed. They saw names, numbers, miles, coordinates.

These individuals, however, are becoming the exception. The norm is the opposite. The problem is no longer a surfeit of information, but a form of proud ignorance. Many travelers know why they are going, but not where they are going. The train, to them, is just an airplane that never takes off.

You can hardly ask a commuter to sit glued to the window in rapt enchantment every day of his life. But when you're somewhere new, looking around is a duty. That's the world out there, and it's putting on a show for us.

//////////////////

You may have noticed, if you read the things I write, that I have the greatest respect for the new Italians. Some of them—if I may transition for a moment from railway metaphors to nautical ones—mistake the harbor for the sea, and take refuge in petty anesthetic habits (their soccer team, their local bar, their friends, their city). But most of them have been obliged to launch their boats just as a storm is hitting—a storm that's been blowing for several years now, and which isn't nearly over.

There are those who insist that millennials—the generation born between 1980 and 2000—are uninformed. Frankly, that doesn't seem to me to be the case. They get their information in an unorthodox manner (Facebook notifications, text messages), while we got our information in a linear manner (radio → TV → daily newspaper → weekly newsmagazine → book). But young people do know things. They know when and why things happen. But they don't always know where.

Ask them to describe the route between Saxony and Castile, or to find Eritrea on a globe. Ask them to list the countries that border Ukraine, or what great river empties into the Black Sea. Ask them to tell you the capitals of Latvia, Cambodia, Paraguay, Nigeria, and New Zealand. And prepare to be surprised: I certainly was. I asked several young people to list the four provincial capitals of Campania and I saw expressions of true anguish. A niece of mine—there are quite a few, so the identity remains vague—once told me how many miles she thought it was from Milan to Paris. I'm not going to tell you her answer, because I love her.

My father, born in 1917, answers these questions without hesitation. His generation had neither Google Maps nor GPS, but they had atlases, teachers, and a certain method. The locating took place in their head;

they had no need of a smartphone. My generation—born in the fifties and sixties of the twentieth century—never had the same level of skill, but maps soothed our unrequited yearnings, and we did learn a little something. I suspect that, in the last twenty years, the socio-politico-economic-environmental teaching of geography might have overlooked some of the basic notions. Where a place is, for instance.

If we don't know where a place is, we'll never fully understand how sweet it is to get there. Or how sad it is to leave, as your train chugs past the last few houses of a city where something important happened.

We'd lose something, and it would be a shame.

Reading

Books are astonishing. They can excite us and keep us up at night. They can depress us and then raise us. They can transport us through time and space, and take us into wonderful worlds. They can give us courage when we most need it. The best ones manage to uplift us and change our moods. These are the perfect books to take with us aboard a train; the therapy of the rails runs through here, too.

Which books are the most tonic? Among the various psychotropic literary substances, these are the hardest to find. A detective novel—be it a thriller, noir, or police procedural—generates tension and inquiry. A family saga draws us in. A love story arouses empathy; if there's sex, curiosity and excitement ensue. These are literary genres with reliable effects. That is why publishers love inspectors, heartthrobs, sighs, and nuances.

Railway fiction is elusive. To start with, it's not universal; everyone has to find their own tonic. I don't recommend professional humorists: all too often, they're depressing. I began, as a teenager, with P. G. Wodehouse, whom I found exhilarating; rereading him today, he strikes me as an autopsy report on a now-dead England. Twenty years later I moved on to Tom Sharpe: no effect. A few minor psychological stirrings—a smile, the desire to pick up the book again—with David Lodge (*Small World, Nice Work, Thinks* . . .). But it wasn't the humor that attracted me. It was something else, and I still can't quite pin it down. Perhaps it was movement, travel, and change.

Are travel books the books you should pack in your suitcase, then? I wouldn't be so sure. Great traveler writers are excellent company if they teach you to travel; otherwise, they're just asking us to admire them for their exploits, their imagination, and their courage. On the Trans-Siberian Railroad, I brought *The Big Red Train Ride* by Eric Newby (appropriately disguised, since it was a prohibited book), a highly informative masterpiece of intelligence and wit that colored my trip from Moscow to Beijing. The most methodical of all the railway authors—Paul Theroux, previously quoted in this book—is on the other hand so very literary and adventurous that he's intimidating. Taking *The Old Patagonian Express* with you on a train from Boston to New York is fair, but perhaps excessive.

On the Web site www.goodreads.com, I found a section devoted to uplifting fiction. It begins with an explanation ("When you close these books you feel happy to be alive, secure that life is worth living"), a warning ("Some of these books may deal with the dark side of life, but they still convey that overall it is good to be alive"), and a ranking. First place goes to *Pride and Prejudice*; third place, *To Kill a Mockingbird*; eighth place, *A Room with a View*; twelfth place, *Life of Pi*; and thirteenth place, *Bridget Jones's Diary*.

Useful references with a view to our imminent departures? Not at all.

Let's try to turn the question around. What authors do I admire without considering them in any way uplifting? Let's stick with the contemporary Brits. Martin Amis and Ian McEwan: exciting and depressing, not particularly encouraging. *The Pregnant Widow* and *Sweet Tooth* have a few moments of happiness: the young English visitors in the castle in Campania, the limited-run love affair of Serena, a student at Cambridge. American authors? Don DeLillo: epic, not especially reassuring. *Underworld* is a masterpiece—it recounts times and places in a sublime manner—but it hardly sprays good humor in all directions. Jonathan Franzen? Brilliant, occasionally therapeutic, but it's a demanding therapy. Nor can the uneasy Philip Roth of the twenty-first century be considered a dispenser of good cheer (the man in question would only take offense). *Everyman* (2006), *Indignation* (2008), *The Humbling* (2009), and *Nemesis* (2010) prepare you to accept death, not to enjoy life. The Zuckerman saga—up to *Exit Ghost*—sounds a different note: a sort of skeptical good humor. Like the Bech series, written by the suave John Updike.

Interesting: I found particularly stimulating those novels that illuminate everyday life with a new light; that suggest a point of view; that put things into a new order. They generate a sense of gratitude: Good job, author! You made yourself useful. You wrote things that I, too, like so many others, had thought, but set out on the page, they acquire a new confirmation.

A book like that—a book capable of uplifting me—was *The World According to Garp*. I read it in 1980, I've reread it, and I've never forgotten it. Paradoxical episodes and grotesque incidents dissolve into the everyday life of the United States, of which John Irving ably transmits the flavor. Pages that taste of cold beer and barbecue sauce, potent evocations of America.

Another American novel functions in a different way but possesses the same degree of psychotropic capacity, and it has only just recently enjoyed a certain success: *Stoner* by John Edward Williams (first published in 1965). The owner of the Elliott Bay Book Company, in Seattle, recommended it to me. After a public event, he came up to me and said: "This is a gift. You'll thank me."

Let me get that out of the way right now: I do thank you. It is a book at once melancholy and happy, a surprising conveyor of serenity. I might recommend it to my seatmate or neighbor on a train, if he or she is behaving well. It tells the story of a teacher in Missouri who tries to give meaning to a life that offers few satisfactions. A life in which, however, he has stuck it out. He has done what he could.

And Italy? One happy book is *Una questione privata* by Beppe Fenoglio, which was published posthumously in 1963, two months after the author's death (and translated into English variously as *A Private Matter*, 1988, and *A Private Affair*, 2007). The book makes you love life the way the young protagonist loved it. The partisan Milton—a young man in the midst of the tempest of the Italian Resistance in World War II—not only explains to us, in simple terms, what a civil war is, but also recounts the beauty of existence, where only a very few would see beauty at all. Fulvia, Giorgio, the hills, the villa, the rain, hard work, youth: it all mingles and takes on meaning.

Another peddler of happiness? Goffredo Parise, who wasn't a happy man. But *Sillabari* (translated into English twice, as *Abecedary*, 1984, and *Solitudes*, 1998) is a sentimental education, a brief history of Italy, and, above all, a lesson: that precious moments are hidden in everyday life, and often we aren't capable of capturing them. "Nowadays, I believe people need feelings more than they do ideologies," Parise explained, right in the midst of an ideological era. The first stories—or poems in prose?—came out in the *Corriere della Sera* between 1971 and 1972, the rest, between 1973 and 1980. Read "Dolcezza" ("Sweetness"). You'll understand what a journey can become, even just a short journey: a few simple touristic pursuits, over the course of a morning in Venice, illuminated by the author's sensibility. Happiness and regret, taken together, produce sweetness: an impeccable title.

A pleasurable nostalgia for time as it passes: this, perhaps, is the hallmark of encouraging books. An author who was endowed with this talent was Mario Soldati. Born in 1906, he was a journalist, a writer, a traveler, and a gourmet *ante litteram*. He died in 1999 at Tellaro near La Spezia, where he had lived for many years. When I first read Soldati, I immediately thought, *This man is a distributor of joy*.

Natalia Ginzburg came to the same conclusion:

Soldati alone among Italian writers of the twentieth century constantly and unfailingly delighted in expressing the joy of living. Not the pleasure of living, but the joy; the pleasure of living is that of the tourist who visits places around the world, savoring their delights and all they have to offer, but overlooking or recoiling from the foul, or sick, or cruel aspects; the joy of living recoils from nothing and no one: it contemplates the universe, explores it in all its misery, and absolves it.

There, perhaps that's the key: a book changes your mood when it says the right thing at the appropriate moment, in a suitable tone. Mario Soldati possessed that key, and he used it to offer access to his world. A world where nature and the word console, where friends fill your life, where departures and arrivals are unforgettable, childhood is a treasure, and wine is a gift.

America First Love was published in 1935, when the author was twenty-nine. A small literary miracle, full of space, promise, and messages:

Certainly, thinking back to Perrero, Praly, and Ghigo, remembering the alpine intoxications of my adolescence, the afternoons stretched out on my belly on the arid, windy ridges, among the schist detritus, and the cobalt blue gentianella, and, far away, in the same glance, the green valleys striped with mountain torrents, the mountaintops of France, the glaciers of Pelvoux; that blazing sun, that violent, icy wind, that torpor, that happiness, the chiming bells of the flocks (little patches of white, still on the distant grassy hillsides), wandering lightly on the wind into the immensity of space, and at times shouts, the lost cries of shepherds, and long high-pitched songs of girls spreading out into the sun and the blue sky, I felt an absolute desire to go back there. But I still didn't know that the only true sin is to ignore or forget that which can make us, each of us, happy.

For his whole life, hidden behind a mustache and a smile, that's the
way Mario Soldati was: caught between Piedmont—to which Liguria
is the elegant briny fringe—and the world, which is why he has never
ceased to surprise himself. A horizontal form of writing that never
intimidates readers, but invites them to draw closer. And, once they are
close enough, whispers to them: *Let me teach you to look; this is how it's done.*

As in "Disco Rosso" (Red Disk), from *La messa dei villeggianti* (The
Vacationers' Mass, 1959). Italy is a spectacle; the railway is the self-
propelled stage of a theater:

> The train slows, awakening me. I raise the shade, look out, and rec-
> ognize the Tuscan countryside, just beyond Arezzo. In the golden
> light of the late summer afternoon, fields, meadows, orchards, for-
> ests, roads, paths, farms, scattered houses, and villas rising high atop
> the hills, everything I see falls magically into order, of a supreme and
> heartbreaking beauty. . . .
>
> A light breeze brushes over the grass on the edges of the tracks.
> Scattered, cheerful voices reach me from the train and from farther
> away, deeper in the countryside. I look at those gentle colors, all the
> greens of all those trees, the green of the olive trees, the green of
> the cypresses, the green of the oaks, the green of the chestnuts,
> and the green of the grass; the yellowish, reddish dirts; the white,
> pink, and gray houses; the sky, clear and a pale blue. I look out at
> that secret geometry, indecipherable and yet perceptible, whereby
> the entire landscape appears to have been constructed like the
> landscape in a canvas by a supremely great painter.
>
> There can be no doubt: happiness, beauty, the meaning of life,
> are here before me. And just as I asked myself when I was young:
> what must I do to be worthy of this beauty, to touch this happiness,
> to understand what the meaning of life is? Likewise, I now ask
> myself, with the same anxiety: what have I done, in all these years,
> to be faithful to the memory of this moment?

More than a book, a pharmaceutical. To be taken before, during, or after a journey, as you prefer. Accompany it with a glass of chilled white wine, in memory of the author.

Writing

Ideas come when they choose. And aboard trains, it is my impression, they often choose to. Dino Buzzati—perhaps Italy's greatest railway poet—was asked, "What is inspiration for you?" and he replied: "It is the idea, the exact idea." A little later, in the same interview, he speaks of "a sort of flame that catches" and he attributes the creative process to "a stranger, a mysterious personage about whom I know very little."

To that elusive individual goes all our admiration as readers in motion. Dino Buzzati understood that every journey is stimulating. Landscapes, faces, new situations, and unusual pairings produce original thoughts.

In this, Buzzati was a past master. The people he glimpsed as his train rolled by on the rails, inside those illuminated windows, can be found in his stories ("Qualcosa era successo," or "Something Had Happened") and in his paintings (*Ragazza che precipita*, or *Falling Girl*). Trains are among the protagonists of his *Poema a fumetti* (*Poem Strip*):

The direct trains the express trains the trains headed for eternity and death depart at fifteen past the 199th hour at two past the zero hour, but where do they go? They go. The rest is the secret of the second life, if there is one, there lies the mystery, the everlasting question. They leave for remote and unknowable destinations. The stationmaster sounds the blessed whistle, the locomotive starts up and puffs smoke, the windows are illuminated, the chefs on the international lines rush to and fro in a flurry of excitement, Toscanini is here, Marilyn is on board, Einstein has just arrived, not to mention

Rene Magritte, hurry, hurry, we're headed toward far-off places. Toward adventure. Toward . . . toward . . .

"You mean toward life?"

"No, no, sorry. All I mean is the steam, the smoke, the speed."

All the author of *The Tartar Steppe* needed was a trolley—rails in the city—to depict Milan.

Aboard the trolley, looking around
he saw drawn grim dead faces
Musocco Inter money
the corrupt intellectual with his hair hanging down his back leaving
    the Bar Giamaica.
Look! The shutters the fines checking the clock
The metal shutter crashing down . . .

But none of us is Buzzati; and few enough, these days, show even traces of that sensibility. One fact remains. Travel in general—travel by train in particular—is a mental fertilizer: it helps ideas to sprout. But you have to tend them if you want them to grow. Imagination requires a certain method.

Here are ten things not to do, when the time comes to invent things.

1. Don't Improvise

Inventing's not the same thing as improvising. It means choosing among ideas. Some ideas are invited with meetings, encounters, images, readings, changes, and travel. Others arrive unlooked for, in the form of illuminations. Illuminations—moments of sudden, surprising clarity—should be taken seriously, the way they are in the comics (lightbulb!). Many will lead nowhere, and occasionally they can even prove embarrassing ("How could I ever have thought such a thing?"). Others, after causing an initial burst of enthusiasm, will turn out to be weak (being able to abandon them is a virtue). But others will bear fruit. Every great adventure of humanity began with a good idea, which someone was able to recognize.

2. Don't Exclude

It's necessary to foster mental associations and emotional contamina- tions. That is why the train—a form of social travel, in contrast with the automobile—helps us to think. Let's say it again: traveling produces stimuli; it brings new experiences; it leads us to take risks—emotional, if no other kind. Without emotions, you execute; you don't invent. If we exclude the new, all that remains is the old—and more or less, we already know that. Not excluding often means including. Let's take the profes- sions of journalist and writer. Nowadays our professional instincts can be put to the test, rapidly and gratuitously. From a tweet or a post that is widely liked and shared, an article can spring, and from the article an investigation, and from the investigation a column, and from the column a book, and in the end from the book, a television program or a play or a one-person show. The public is an excellent coauthor. Sometimes it's ferocious, quite often too generous. But it's never fraudulent.

3. Don't Fool Yourself

Avoid overweening ambition and pride. Examine new ideas with a realistic eye, and ward off the interferences of passion: not everything we like is opportune, or necessarily within our reach. Creativity—like seduction and modern art, and unlike the tango, swimming, and billiards—allows us to bluff, even with ourselves. Writing, in particular, pushes us toward dangerous illusions that other professions don't allow. Here, once again, is the importance of society—even the microcosm enclosed inside a moving train—and of social media. They're an important test, a freezer to calm down unjustified bursts of heat. If no one gives any sign of being impressed with your stories, don't you begin to wonder whether you might not know how to write? In order to take on new challenges, moreover, it's wise to be convinced of what you're doing: you need to learn how, and that takes time. Being adventurous is admirable; being conceited is annoying.

4. Don't Get Sloppy

Avoid sloppiness, approximation, and excessive haste. You need to work gradually and with precision on your projects (there's a difference between precision and nit-picking: nitpickers are pedantic; the precise are romantic). Make notes of your ideas, correct them, and improve them. Work on the details. Many creative projects, before they are completed, may appear confused. Instead they are excellent; all they need is some work. A patient imagination may seem, to some, like a contradiction in terms. However, it's a virtue that brings results. The initial illumination is defined, refined, and polished. Every trip, in its way, is an odyssey. But before making it something that can be spelled with a capital letter, someone worked for a very long time on the Odyssey.

5. Don't Be Afraid

Many of us, when visiting new places and doing different things, are afraid of scattering our energy and attention. The question that many ask themselves is this: does trying lots of things help or distract? Answer: it helps, as long as we are disciplined (see point 4). Every trip you take, every person you meet, and every new experience is a source of knowledge. Reality is creative by definition. But some of us prefer the pond of habit to the river of life (and then they complain about the toads).

6. Don't Copy

Do original ideas exist? Albert Einstein is supposed to have said, ironically: "The secret to creativity is knowing how to hide your sources." There's some truth to that: knowledge is contamination and progress.

We are the consequence of those who went before us. Life is borrowed and the world is borrowed. Not stolen, though. Imitation and inspiration lead to invention by being tuned in. A writer reads to find the right frequency. One phrase suggests other phrases; an image suggests other images; a place, other places. That's normal. Those who write have to read; those who sing or play an instrument have to listen; those who paint have to look. Beware of cooks with no appetite.

7. Don't Force Things

Original ideas, we've said, don't come on command. And they don't arrive if our brain is constantly occupied, like the bathrooms at the roadside grills on summer highways. Bain & Company, a consulting firm, has calculated the number of messages we each receive: a thousand a year in 1970, roughly thirty thousand today. Ideas have to find a breach in this forest of stimuli and information. The best moments? On trains, as this book suggests (and during travel in general, especially when we don't have to drive, navigate, and decide). When you're sleepy and during long meetings (the two things often seem to coincide). Showers, beaches, gyms. There's no point in insisting on this point: there is no such thing as an automatic vending machine for ideas. They come willingly only when we're not phoning, answering, posting, chatting. Adrenaline is STP for the engines of healthy people, but calm, pauses, and rest are indispensable. Invention is like sex: if you're preoccupied, it doesn't work.

8. Don't Be Distracted

Robert M. Pirsig writes in *Zen and the Art of Motorcycle Maintenance*: "Some things you miss because they're so tiny you overlook them. But some things you don't see because they're so huge." Creative people don't allow themselves to be distracted: their antennae are always functioning. They're capable of drawing inspiration from anything. In every field, nowadays, what counts is the angle, the style, the packaging of a proposal. We journalists often forget this. We used to believe that being on a prestigious masthead was enough. When the Internet, the great disrupter, made much content easily accessible and free, certain products showed their limitations. If we're not capable of adapting, it won't be the end of the world, just the end of an industry. By now it ought to be clear: if you don't supply value, you're worthless. And if you're worthless, you won't survive.

9. Don't Isolate Yourself

In order to create, you need to mix: talents and personalities, expertise and generations. Certain combinations—experience and enthusiasm, prudence and recklessness, caution and spontaneity—allow us to go far. A fifty-year-old and a twenty-year-old are natural allies: each possesses what the other lacks. Often the former contributes method, self-control, and the ability to synthesize; the latter, almost invariably, brings the gifts of energy, recklessness, and originality.

Steve Jobs believed in variety. He called biologists, mathematicians, writers, and a jurist (though not more than one!) to the working groups at Apple. In a *New York Times* op-ed piece, Laszlo Bock, the senior vice president of people operations for Google, explained the characteristics he's looking for in new hires: "The No. 1 thing we look for is general cognitive ability, and it's not I.Q. It's learning ability. It's the ability to process on the fly. It's the ability to pull together disparate bits of information. The second is leadership. When you're a member of a team, do you, at the appropriate time, step in and lead? And just as critically, do you step back and stop leading, do you let someone else?" In California, just as anywhere else, companies, nowadays, aren't interested in knowing where, how, and what you studied. They want to know what you learned.

10. Don't Become Rigid

Constrained creativity is an oxymoron, but organizations aren't convinced. Peter Drucker—a guru of corporate management, born in Vienna in 1909, a naturalized American—once said: "So much of what we call management consists in making it difficult for people to work." A paradox that is as relevant as ever: the rigid division between inventors and implementers is a grotesque thing. In *La chiave a stella* (*The Monkey's Wrench*, or *The Wrench*), Primo Levi describes, with intelligence and love, a phenomenon that many of us notice every day: the brilliance of manual labor. If publishers had the ability to analyze the elasticity and the precision of a carpenter or a farmer, books would be greatly improved.

////////////////

Invention and organization aren't incompatible. They are, in fact, complementary. "Power is nothing without control," reads the headline of an ad campaign for tires. The same applies to the world of ideas. Method without imagination leads to boredom. Imagination without method leads to derailment. And such a thing can't happen, not at the end of a book like this one.

ACKNOWLEDGMENTS

This isn't a travel book; it's a book that travels. Some of the sections you've read here were conceived aboard trains, while the events were occurring; the landscapes were changing; the passengers were speaking. My first acknowledgment, then, goes to the various railways— Italian, German, European, American, Australian. Even Soviet railways, in the mid-1980s. They took me safe and sound to my destination; they gave me plots, characters, opportunities, and emotions.

I'm a journalist: this is not a work of fiction; the stories I tell here really happened.

Each time, someone proved to be particularly important, and I want to give thanks here.

My first thank-you goes to my son, Antonio, who took his dad across America. As you've read, we left Washington, DC, and we arrived, overland, in Washington State in the summer of 2013. Traveling with a twenty-year-old son is an immense privilege. You're awesome, kid.

My warmest thanks go to my wife. Ortensia put up with me from Moscow to Beijing (an uncomfortable but unforgettable honeymoon, in 1986) and from Helsinki to Istanbul in the summer of 1989, while Communism was crumbling (at last!) all around us. She proved to be an amazing traveler; she still is.

My traveling companions in Italy—Soledad Ugolinelli and Gianni Scimone—were also with me from Berlin to Palermo (2010), from

Moscow to Lisbon (2011), and from the Atlantic to the Pacific (2012). I talk about them in the book, and I'll add nothing except for this: thank you, I'd go with you to the ends of the earth (truth be told, we already have!). Traveling with us were Mark Spörrle (2010 and 2011) and Karl Hoffmann (2012). I thank them both for having put up with me and for showing that Germans, contrary to the stereotypes, are unpredictable.

One last thank-you—obligatory, sincere, and heartfelt—goes to Susanne Höhn and the Goethe-Institut. They gave me a chance to tell the story of Italy, Europe, and America, they gave me their trust, and they gave me their friendship, something every bit as important. Another partner in these three journeys was the *Corriere della Sera*; also, on the American trip, the television network La7. For the rail trip from Sydney to Perth (2007), thanks again to the *Corriere*, to Tourism Australia, and to the Italian Cultural Institutes down under.

Finally, let me also thank two Americans, quite different from each other. The first is President Donald Trump, who traveled with me from Naples to London in the fall of 2017 (but only as a statuette—which is good, as he didn't tweet, complain, attack, or fire anyone). The second is my patient, talented, and resourceful translator, Antony Shugaar. It is our first book together, and it was great to see him in action. I write my journalism in English, not my books. I can appreciate a good translation, though. And Tony's is excellent.

A final thought goes to my friend Giles Watson, the translator of three of my books into English, who is no longer with us. I owe him a lot. This book is dedicated to him.

INDEX OF PLACES

Abilene, Texas, 21
Abruzzo, Italy, 137
Achinsk, Russia, 154
Acireale, Sicily, 144
Acquaviva delle Fonti, Italy, 140
Adelaide, South Australia, 84, 86–88, 91
Adriatic Sea, 127, 136–39
Alabama, U.S., 8, 11, 12
Albany, New York, 100–3
Alexandria, Louisiana, 18
Alice Springs, Australia, 87
Alpharetta, Georgia, 11, 179, 181
Amherst, New Hampshire, 96
Amsterdam, the Netherlands, 100
Anaheim, California, 37
Apennines Mountains, 136
Aragon, Spain, 78
Arizona, U.S., 3, 12, 27–35, 77
Aterno River valley, 137
Atlanta, Georgia, 3, 8, 10, 11, 100, 125
Atlantic Ocean, xiv, 42, 79, 96, 98, 101, 103, 117, 119, 121
Austin, Texas, 12, 106
Australia, xv, 19, 83–93, 100, 128
Austria, 50, 60, 65, 69–72, 127, 129
Aztec, New Mexico, 33

Baltic Sea, xiv
Baltimore, Maryland, 7, 10, 100
Barcelona, Spain, 75–78, 81
Bari, Italy, 139, 140

Basilicata, Italy, 141
Baton Rouge, Louisiana, 18
Bavaria, 49–50
Bega, New South Wales, 85
Beijing, China, xiv, 54, 59, 150, 155, 158, 167, 189
Belarus, 164
Belgrade, Yugoslavia, 173
Benevento, Italy, 137, 139
Benghazi, Libya, 77
Berkeley, California, 40
Berlin, Germany, 43–46, 52, 57, 58, 168, 170–72, 174
Bern, Switzerland, 72
Birmingham, Alabama, 8, 12
Black Forest, 118
Black Sea, 187
Blue Mountains, 85
Bogotol, Russia, 154
Bohemia, Czech Republic, 68, 69
Bolzano, Italy, 52, 53
Bookaloo, Australia, 88
Bordeaux, France, 76
Bosphorus, xiv, 159
Boston, Massachusetts, 10, 95–100, 103, 108, 161, 189
Brazil, 77
Brenner Pass, 52
Brescia, Italy, 91, 129
Brindisi, Italy, 136
British Columbia, Canada, 42

Broken Hill, Australia, 86
Budapest, Hungary, 67, 172
Buffalo, New York, 103
Bulgaria, 173–75

Calabria, Italy, 55–57, 141–43
California, U.S., 3, 4, 21, 34–39, 98, 100,
    122, 124, 125
Caltanissetta Xirbi, Sicily, 146
Cambodia, 187
Campania, Italy, 139, 187
Canada, 100, 108
Canyon de Chelly, Arizona, 31
Cascade Range, 120
Castle of Miramare, 129
Catania, Sicily, 143, 145
Catanzaro, Italy, 142
Cerkezköv, Turkey, 175
Charlotte, North Carolina, 8
Chicago, Illinois, 104, 106–8, 122
Chico, California, 39
Chihuahua Desert, Texas, 24
China, xiii, 59, 100, 150, 155,
    157–58
Cisco, Texas, 23
Ciudad Juárez, Mexico,
    26–27
Cleveland, Ohio, 102–4
Clyde, Texas, 23
Cochise County, Arizona, 28
Columbia River, 120
Cook, Australia, 88
Costa del Sol, 67
Crema, Italy, 2, 100, 143
Cremona, Italy, 29, 129
Crotone, Italy, 56
Cuyahoga River, 104
Czech Republic, 60, 65–68, 71
Czechoslovakia, 175

Dallas, Texas, 3, 20–21
Danilov, Russia, 152
Darwin, Australia, 88
Dateland, Arizona, 33
Dauriya, Russia, 157
Descanso, California, 34

Devils Lake, North Dakota, 112
District of Columbia, U.S., 3–6, 10, 42,
    100, 124

Edirne, Turkey, 175
Edmonds, Washington, 120
Egypt, 47
El Paso, Texas, 26
El Salvador, 27
England, 65, 119, 134, 177,
    183–84
Enna, Sicily, 145, 146
Erie Canal, 103
Estremadura province, Portugal, 82
Eugene, Oregon, 41
Everett, Washington, 120, 121

Fargo, North Dakota, 110
Figueres, Spain, 81
Finland, 159–62, 175
Flagstaff, Arizona, 3, 32
Flensburg, Germany, 49
Florence, Italy, 133, 134, 138
Florida, U.S., 98, 100
Foggia, Italy, 137, 138
Foligno, Italy, 136
Fort Apache, Arizona, 31
France, 60, 65, 72–76, 80, 81, 180,
    182–83, 187
Frankfurt an der Oder, Germany, 170
Fulda, Germany, 48
Fullerton, California, 37

Gargano Promontory, 138
Geneva, Switzerland, 72, 81
Genoa, Italy, 131–32
Georgia, U.S., 3, 8, 10–11, 100, 111,
    179, 181
Germany, 43–52, 50, 64–65, 67, 72,
    170–72, 175
Giardini Naxos, Sicily, 144
Gila Bend, Arizona, 33
Gioia del Colle, Italy, 140
Glacier National Park, 117
Gleeson, Arizona, 28
Göttingen, Germany, 47

Grand Cane, Louisiana, 18
Grand Canyon, Arizona, 12
Great Lakes, 103
Greenville, South Carolina, 10
Grodno, Belarus, 167
Gross Tete, Louisiana, 18
Guatemala, 27
Gulf of Finland, 161
Gulf of Mexico, 42

Hamburg, Germany, 67
Helsinki, Finland, 159, 160, 175
Honduras, 27
Horn of Africa, 97
Hötensleben, Germany, 47
Houston, Texas, 104
Hudson River, 103
Hungary, 67, 105, 175

Icicle Canyon, 120
Idaho, U.S., 114, 118
Illinois, U.S., 104, 106–8, 122
India, xiii
Indian Ocean, 90
Indiana, U.S., 106
Inner Mongolia, 158
Innsbruck, Austria, 70, 71
Ionian Sea, 140, 141, 143
Irkutsk, Russia, 153, 155, 156
Irvine, California, 37
Irving, Texas, 21
Ishim, Russia, 154
Istanbul, Turkey, 159, 175
Italy, 48, 52–56, 72, 91, 127–44, 148,
    177–81, 187, 191–93, 195

Jackson, Mississippi, 19
Japan, 100
Jilin province, China, 158

Kalgoorlie, Western Australia,
88–89
Kama River, 152
Kapikule, Turkey, 175
Kiev, Ukraine, 62–63, 71
Kingman, Arizona, 30

Kingoonya, Australia, 88
Kirov, Russia, 152
Klamath Falls, Oregon, 39, 41
Kouvola, Finland, 160
Kraków, Poland, 64, 66, 67, 70, 71, 77
Krasnoyarsk, Russia, 155
Kultanaby, Australia, 88
Kutno, Poland, 168
Kuznica Bialostocka, Poland, 167

La Joya, Texas, 27
Lafayette, Louisiana, 18
Lake Baikal, 153, 156
Lake Erie, 104, 106
Lake McDonald, 117
Lake Washington, 123, 124
Lamezia Terme, Italy, 55–56
L'Aquila, Italy, 136
Las Vegas, Nevada, 38
Latvia, 164, 166, 187
Lausanne, Switzerland, 72
Lazio (Latium), Italy, 136
Leningrad, Russia, 160, 162–64
Liguria, Italy, 131–33, 193
Ligurta, Arizona, 33
Linz, Austria, 70
Lisbon, Portugal, 59, 81, 82, 110
Lithuania, 164, 167
Liverpool, England, 119
Livorno, Italy, 92, 133–34, 137
Locri, Italy, 142
Lombardy, 129
London, England, 100, 177, 183–84
Longview, Texas, 20
Lordsburg, New Mexico, 28
Los Angeles, California, 3, 4, 37,
    100, 124
Louisiana, U.S., 3, 7, 8, 13–14, 18, 19
Lower Saxony, Germany, 46
Luzhaika, Finland, 161
Lyon, France, 72–74, 81, 180

Madrid, Spain, 78–81
Maiella Mountains, 137
Maine, U.S., 95–97, 125
Malta, Montana, 113–16, 123

Manchuria, China, 156
Mantua, Italy, 83, 129–30
Many Farms, Arizona, 31
Manzhouli, China, 157
Maralinga, Australia, 88
Maritsa River, 174
Marsala, Sicily, 147
Marseille, France, 73–75, 80, 81
Marshall, Texas, 20
Maryland, U.S., 7, 10, 100
Massachusetts, U.S., 18, 95–100
Mazara, Sicily, 147
Melbourne, Australia, 83, 91
Meridian, Mississippi, 12
Mesquite, Texas, 20
Messina, Sicily, 57, 143, 144
Metaponto, Italy, 141
Mexico, 26–27
Miami, Florida, 98, 100
Milan, Italy, 54, 57, 118, 177, 187, 195
Milwaukee, Wisconsin, 103, 108–10
Mississippi River, 14
Mississippi State, U.S., 12, 14, 19
Modane, France, 180
Modena, Italy, 52, 54, 130
Moldau River, 67
Molise, Italy, 138
Montana, U.S., 111, 113–19, 123
Monte Giano, 136
Montpellier, France, 76, 81
Montreal, Canada, 100
Moscow, Russia, 59–62, 70–71, 110, 119,
   149–51, 153, 156
Moskva River, 62
Mount Rainier, 122
Munich, Germany, 48, 50, 172

Naples, Italy, 54, 55, 57
Navajo National Monument,
   31–32
New England, U.S., 95
New Hampshire, U.S., 95
New Mexico, U.S., 27–28, 33
New Orleans, Louisiana, 3, 7, 8,
   13–14
New South Wales, Australia, 85, 86

New York, New York, 4, 7, 10, 100–3, 122
New York State, 4, 7, 10, 100–3, 122
New Zealand, 91, 187
Niagara Falls, 106
Nice, France, 73
Nigeria, 187
Niš, Serbia, 173
Norfolk Island, Australia, 87
North Carolina, U.S., 8
North Dakota, U.S., 110–14
Novoselye, Russia, 165
Novosibirsk, Russia, 154
Nullarbor Plain, Australia, 84, 88

Oakland, California, 39
Oceanside, California, 37
Oder River, 170
Odessa, Texas, 23
Ohio, U.S., 102–6
Olovyannaya, Russia, 156, 157
Olympia, Washington, 42
Olympic Mountains, 122
Onon River, 157
Ooldea, Australia, 88
Opelousas, Louisiana, 18
Oregon, U.S., 39–41, 96, 120, 121, 125
Ostrov, Russia, 165
Ottawa, Canada, 100

Pacific Ocean, 34, 96, 120, 121, 150, 156
Padua, Italy, 138
Painted Desert, 31
Palermo, Sicily, 57, 58, 145–47
Palma de Mallorca, Spain, 75
Paraguay, 187
Paris, France, 180, 182–83, 187
Parma, Italy, 138
Patti, Sicily, 58
Pavia, Italy, 138
Pecos, Texas, 24
Pennsylvania, U.S., 7, 10, 100
Perm, Russia, 152
Perth, Western Australia, 83, 84, 88, 90–93
Perugia, Italy, 135–36, 138
Pescara, Italy, 136–38
Petrified Forest, 31

Philadelphia, Pennsylvania, 7, 10, 100
Phoenix, Arizona, 30, 33, 77
Piacenza, Italy, 32, 130, 131, 138
Piedmont, Italy, 193
Pisa, Italy, 138
Pistoia, Italy, 138
Pittsfield, Massachusetts, 100
Plovdiv, Bulgaria, 174
Poland, 64, 70, 71, 77, 163, 164, 166–70, 175
Polebridge, Montana, 118
Port Augusta, Australia, 87
Portland, Maine, 95–97, 125
Portland, Oregon, 41, 96, 120, 121, 125
Portugal, 59, 60, 65, 81, 82
Poznan, Poland, 168, 171
Prague, Czech Republic, 65–68, 71
Pskov, Russia, 165
Puget Sound, 121, 122
Puglia, Italy, 129, 140

Qatar, 47

Redding, California, 39
Reggio Calabria, Italy, 142, 143
Repino, Russia, 162
Rezekne, Latvia, 166
Rhône River, 81
Rieti, Italy, 136
Rio de Janeiro, Brazil, 77
Rio Grande, 26, 27
Rocky Mountains, 117
Romanengo, Italy, 100
Romania, 105, 175
Rome, Italy, 55, 57, 119, 138, 177, 179
Rosarno, Italy, 143
Rough Rock, Arizona, 31
Rugby, North Dakota, 110, 112–13
Russia, 59–62, 70–71, 110, 119, 149–57, 161–65, 175

Sacramento, California, 39
Salzburg, Austria, 70, 71
San Diego, California, 3, 21, 34–35, 98, 100
San Francisco, California, 3, 100, 122
San Juan Capistrano, California, 37

San Luis Obispo, California, 38
Sankt Anton am Arlberg, Austria, 70, 71
Santa Ana, California, 37
Santa Barbara, California, 37
Santa Maria Novella, Italy, 134
Santa Monica, California, 125
Santa Teresa di Riva, Sicily, 144
Sardinia, 15–16
Savannah, Georgia, 111
Saxony, Germany, 46, 47
Scandinavia, 65
Sea of Marmara, 175
Seattle, Washington, 3, 42, 114, 119–24
Sentinel, Arizona, 33
Serbia, 173
Shreveport, Louisiana, 19
Sibari, Italy, 142
Siberia, 47, 150, 153–55
Sicily, 57–58, 129, 141, 143–48
Silvi Marina, Italy, 137
Skykomish, Washington, 120
Snohomish River, 121
Sofia, Bulgaria, 174
Solana Beach, California, 37
South America, 47, 77
South Australia, 84, 86–88, 91
South Carolina, U.S., 10
South Korea, 100
Spain, 60, 75–81
Spokane, Washington, 118–20
Springfield, Massachusetts, 100
Strugi Krasnye, Russia, 165
Stuttgart, Germany, 45
Sulmona, Italy, 136, 137
Sverdlovsk, Russia, 153
Svilengrad, Bulgaria, 174
Swiebodzin, Poland, 168, 170
Switzerland, 53, 60, 70–72, 81
Sydney, Australia, 83, 84, 88, 91

Tacna, Arizona, 33
Tacoma, Washington, 42
Tagus River, 82
Tallapoosa, Georgia, 11
Taranto, Italy, 140–41, 143

Tarcoola, Australia, 88
Tatar Pazardzhik, Bulgaria, 173, 174
Tayshet, Russia, 155
Termini Imerese, Sicily, 146
Termoli, Italy, 138
Terni, Italy, 136
Texas, U.S., 3, 18, 20–24, 26, 27, 104
Theba, Arizona, 33
Tijuana, Mexico, 27
Toledo, Ohio, 106
Tombstone, Arizona, 28–29
Toronto, Canada, 100
Trapani, Sicily, 128, 136, 138, 146–48
Trebisacce, Italy, 142
Trento, Italy, 53, 54
Trieste, Italy, 127–28, 131, 133,
   138, 148
Tucson, Arizona, 3, 27–30
Turin, Italy, 180
Turkey, 159, 175
Tuscaloosa, Alabama, 11
Tuscany, 133–35
Tyler, Texas, 20
Tyrrhenian Sea, 56, 136, 137, 139

Ukraine, 60, 62–64, 71, 187
Umbria, Italy, 136
United States of America, 1–42, 95–125

Vainikkala, Finland, 160
Vancouver, Canada, 42

Venice, Italy, 129, 138
Ventura, California, 37
Verona, Italy, 54
Vienna, Austria, 65, 69, 70
Vietnam, 102
Villa San Giovanni, Italy, 56, 57, 143
Vilnius, Lithuania, 167
Vistula River, 168
Vladivostok, Russia, 153, 156
Voghera, Italy, 131
Volga River, 152
Vyborg (Viipuri), Finland, 161, 162

Warsaw, Poland, 163, 164, 166–68
Washington, D.C., 3–6, 10, 42, 100, 124
Washington State, U.S., 3, 42, 114, 118–24
Weimar, Germany, 47
Western Australia, 83, 84, 88–93
Wielkopolska, Poland, 170
Williston, North Dakota, 112, 114
Winema National Forest, 40
Wirraminna, Australia, 88
Wisconsin, U.S., 108–10
Wolfsburg, Germany, 46, 52

Yenisey River, 155
Yugoslavia, 105, 172, 173
Yuma, Arizona, 33–34

Zabaykalsk, Russia, 157
Zurich, Switzerland, 70–71, 77, 81